FEARLESS PARENTING

Raising Your Child
with
Confidence and Purpose

Adelaide
Zindler, FP

Fearless Parenting
by Adelaide Zindler, FP

David Bauer Press
826 E. Charleston Blvd.
Las Vegas, Nevada 89104

ISBN-13: 978-0-9797119-0-9
Library of Congress Control Number: 2007907198

Disclaimer
The examples provided in this book are for your general knowledge. Concerns about a medical condition, either your own or that of a family member, should always be prayerfully addressed along with a qualified provider for advice and care appropriate to your specific needs. The Fearless Parenting Institute, LLC does not recommend self-diagnosis or self-management of health problems that should be addressed by medical professionals. The views and opinions expressed are those of the author. Any person relying on such information obtained from this book, does so at his or her own risk.

printed in the United States of America

CONTENTS

FOREWORD

Adelaide is an extraordinarily perceptive and creative *Preschool and Family Life Coach* for parents and children. She has a power-packed degree in Child Development, which landed her a position on the well-established Pediatric Health Education team at Palomar-Pomerado Hospital. By identifying the repeated parental patterns (both positive and negative) that occur in family relationships, she pierced the core of parent-child problems. She used this knowledge to design a highly effective preschool model for perinatal substance-abusing parents and their children—a project that was sponsored by Mental Health Systems.

Adelaide Zindler believes that all children are created for greatness. Using this as a core concept, she provides parents with tools that empower them to transform dysfunctional patterns of parenting into functional ones. For example, Adelaide coined the word "*frizzamyer*" to replace the negative labels placed on children. The word denotes the desperate ways parents and children have of expressing their need to be heard and respected.

In Adelaide's programs, she provides a non-judgmental process that allows parents to discover what has worked, what has not worked, and the reasons why. She helps parents switch from emotional reaction to cognitive problem solving. She invites each family to direct their own journey by asking them to identify problematic areas, formulate solutions, practice the solutions, and keep track of the outcomes.

Adelaide's well-woven questions require parents to become active leaders in the process of change. She has compassion for parents who revert to complaining and blaming, and she always brings them back to their long-term goals, never judging or evaluating them. By helping parents stay with the process, Adelaide enables them to maintain healthy control over parent/child interactions that seemed so hopeless before. In this way, the needs of both the parent and child are identified and met. The life-supporting parent/child balance is restored without risking any long-term negative side effects.

Recently, the local media has made a great effort to ensure that the San Diego community knows about Adelaide's programs. She has appeared in interviews on several San Diego news shows. Her concepts have appeared in a variety of print media in the San Diego community and the benefits of her work are currently being promoted by leading child-centered professionals.

Adelaide also developed the Fearless Parenting Institute LLC, also known as *Pre-school and Family Life Coaching*. The core concept of this program is that the child is not the problem. This approach is designed to help parents explore their core values and moral instincts and gain insight into how those beliefs rightly or wrongly affect their parenting practices. Adelaide sets about taking the anger out of communications by creating new words, *words* not contaminated by judgment, but that communicate the complex feelings of both the parent and child.

Those who have experienced the extraordinary abilities of Adelaide depart from her programs with a deep sense of wellbeing, new parenting skills, and an increased confidence in their abilities as parents.

Diane Evans, Ph.D
Child Development Specialist
Mission Valley Mental Health Services

ACKNOWLEDGMENTS

This is a deep subject for me. It is not possible for me to recall all of the people that played a role in the completion of this project, most of whom had no idea of their effect on my life's work. Aside from a few names that I've withheld, I have made an attempt at remembering those who nudged this work along.

Thank you to:

My grandparents, who, during my early childhood, kicked off my speaking career before hundreds of people and convinced me that the sky was my only limit—if that.

My mother, who taught me what being a child should feel like and who forced me to rewrite my homework whether I concurred or not.

All those nameless people whose words have prompted me to keep reviewing the tenets by which I have chosen to live.

My clients, who graciously shared their lives with me and, in so doing, revealed areas in my own life that were excellent or in need of some improvement, and those who read this book and provided feedback to make this edition an even better product than the first.

My numerous associates and colleagues who reviewed this document and became the think-tank in which it was safe to test my thoughts. My Christian writer's critique group, who welcomed me into their organization—and continually surprise Peter and me by supporting our speaking engagements. Thanks guys!

Stewart Title Company—run by another female business owner who was willing to help this female business owner find her footing. Now how American is that?

Stu Segall Productions who caught the vision for this book empowering preschool families, and who willingly got behind it with Mike and their whole team: for rolling out the red carpet for me like they would the star of a blockbuster hit.

My inner circle of trustworthy friends, who walked with me mile after mile (some even literally).

Antoinette and and Jared of Strategies Public Relations for being friends in the process of drawing out of me so much suppressed pain in getting to the root of what makes this message a powerful one. For painstakingly mulling over every line and sharing the journey as if it were their own. I received coaching, book doctoring, and delectable food for thought. I will remain indebted to them for removing some of my own fears in the interest of those who are called to be powerful parents.

Robert Goodman for graciously stepping in at the last minute to see to it that this manuscript went to press before the deadline, and in way better shape than it was in when it was first presented to him. He's an honorary Fearless Parent and a stellar gentleman if ever I met one!

Dr. Timothy and Betty Winters, who provided a spiritual refuge for my family to help us recover our strength, along with their purpose-driven team of Ushers who got us off the bench so that we could also contribute to the Bayview Product. They rock as shepherds!

America's military forces everywhere, who afford me the personal luxury of a life of freedom; who, with high principle, go where they are sent. Some of whose families may never know the magnitude of the way of life that they sacrifice to preserve for us in America, because their chosen vocation prohibits them from fully experiencing it. Who assume a mission that often means being despised at home more than abroad; and who still willingly put themselves in harm's way without one word about the view from their perspective.

My children, who taught me (with compassion) how to meet their needs, and who embraced me so tenderly. They have made motherhood such an extraordinary calling in my life.

I also want to thank the one person who took the time to point me toward higher ground, who showed me that the future held promises worth reaching for, who lived out his faith so that I could touch it, and who held me as I squirmed and fought against it while still loving me unconditionally. He made a gentleman of our son and a virtuous young princess of our daughter. For some 18 years of marriage to my beloved husband and best friend Peter, I could almost write another book called *How to Love a Woman into What You Want Her to Be*.

Of course, I have saved the very best for last: The One without whom my life would still be meaningless, Who made me give back my master's degree in depression, Who showed me that the world did not revolve around me but that I was created to help others climb up to see the breathtaking view, Who made me feel like a princess in His presence, Who sent people to impact my life and me theirs—my Creator and Father Who holds me more closely throughout each scene of my life's play.

THE *ADELOGIC* ACTION PLAN

"The unexamined life is not worth living."
—Socrates

Thank you for purchasing *Fearless Parenting*. If you are new to life coaching, this *Adelogic Action Plan* will provide you with a fresh approach to maximizing your reading experience. Here are some questions that I have designed to help you get the greatest benefit out of our time together. Before you delve into the chapters, preview the questions that follow, and then afterward, return to this section to complete the questions and begin implementing this plan in your life. Welcome to the land of Fearless Parenting!

1. What prompted you to choose this particular book?
2. What are you expecting to gain from this investment of your time?
3. How will your family life change as a result of implementing these Adelogic concepts in your home?

On the next page is the Adelogic action plan that you will see developed throughout this book, along with the chapters where you will find the pieces that will bring this concept together for you.

Adelogic Precepts to Consider		
Chapter 1	Getting Started-Is Preschool the Answer for ALL?	
Chapter 2	Adelogic Your Parenting Style…	A
Chapter 3	Create and Sustain a Strong Family	D
Chapter 4	Empower Your Child Beyond Inhibitions	E
Chapter 5	Learn to Think Past the School Setting	L
Chapter 6	Motivation is More Caught Than Taught	O
Chapter 7	Get Engaged in What Truly Inspires	G
Chapter 8	Teach Them to Fail Forward	I
Chapter 9	Steer Your Family's Ship into Safe Harbor	C
Chapter 10	Growing a Fear-Free Family	

These are three of the goals I now have for improving our home/family life.

1. ______________________________

2. ______________________________

3. ______________________________

Here are the steps I plan to take to achieve these objectives.

I will finish reading this book by:

Date ____________________________Time ___________

I will begin taking action on:

Date ____________________________Time ___________

I will complete this plan on:

Date ____________________________Time ___________

This is how I will celebrate my accomplishment:

1

GETTING STARTED
Is Preschool the Answer for ALL?

There is a move abroad to make preschool mandatory for all children. Not the preschool of the last century, not even the preschool of the last decade, but preschool which begins as soon as, if not before, children begin to speak and continues until they reach kindergarten.

To understand the movement, we have to take into account why this has become an imperative. Several reasons come to mind:

- **Working mothers** – In more and more families, both parents work, therefore requiring safe caretaking for their children.
- **Single family households** – With a large percentage of households now having only one parent, whether due to divorce or unmarried parenthood, single working parents need safe caretaking for their children.
- **Academic competition**—The number of young people applying to colleges has made getting on to

preferred campuses a tremendous challenge. Thus, parents are starting earlier and earlier to channel their children into education.

- **Equalization**—Children come from a variety of socio-economic and educational backgrounds. The theory is that if we begin educating them all equally earlier, it will level the playing field.
- **Weak educational system**—The American educational system is weak. Our children routinely fail to perform up to levels of children in less affluent societies. Parents are persuaded to believe that preschool for all will create better students and thus better overall educational results. Sign up for Club Fearless—the Blog at *www.fearlessparenting.com* and get the facts.

While the list of reasons for preschool can go on and on, the questions remain. Why are we putting pressure on the youngest among us to perform academically? When did options like in-home family childcare, playgroups and the host other part-time options become inferior to full-time institutional state preschools? And does preschool work as well it's touted to? The statistics say no!

More than 5,000 children are expelled from preschool each year

Are children out of control?

Are preschools simply serving more at-risk kids than they did in the past?

Or is our preschool model to blame?

While some children do challenge us more than others, based on the latest brain research, our preschool model is woefully inadequate to fulfill the insatiable developmental appetites of most young children. We are all born with our own Einstein-like capacity with which to explore the vast treasures awaiting our discovery in this wonderful world, using our own unique intelligence. I have yet to find a walled-in room that can house the resources necessary to nurture that potential.

The first five years of a child's development are crucial. They are also a time of constant flux—a time when there are no precise predictors of emotional, intellectual, or social readiness for structured learning. In our push to academically fast-track our children into better long-term performance, we are failing to account for their varying stages of readiness. In the long run, it is emotional and social development that will in part support intellectual achievement!

Statistics suggest that the national push for preschool may be misguided—that if, instead, parents take a more active role in overseeing the emotional, social, intellectual, and spiritual development of their children through age 4, these children will be better prepared for success in grades K-12.

Let's go back to the statement that began this section. More than 5000 children are expelled from preschool each year. That number fails to take into account those diagnosed with learning disabilities, behavioral problems, and those put on adult medications to alleviate them. It fails to take into account the long-term effects of telling a toddler he or she isn't good enough to perform in a situation for which they are not emotionally, socially, intellectually, or spiritually ready. It does not take into account the long-term effects of a child being labeled at 3 years of age with a disorder that will haunt the rest of their academic career.

We know that children benefit from intellectual stimulation; that they learn very rapidly during their first five years; and that those are the years during which much of their character is formed. How does a parent, busy with work and providing for their family, ensure that the needs of their preschool age child are met without putting them into stressful and potentially damaging situations?

Perhaps the first step is to ask if it is really necessary to leave a very young child with a caretaker other than a parent. If the child is from a two-parent family, the question arises as to priorities and whether with a realignment of those, one parent can become the primary caretaker – or how both parents can share the job together.

Still, for many families the choice to have both parents work full-time remains preferable. Whatever the reason for delegating your caretaker role to someone else, on an individual basis parents need to choose child care carefully. They need to assess the programs to which they are considering exposing their children and make certain that those programs fit not just their child's emotional, intellectual, physical, and spiritual needs, but that the programs also are in sync with the life philosophy of the family.

On a societal level, we have to look first at why we are buying into actors' and politicians' ideas and ideals of universal preschool; what it accomplishes; and what it does not. And we have to consider revamping both the preschool experience and our expectations so that they come into agreement with the children being served.

One way to do this is to look again at our attitude toward children in general and preschool children in particular. Our educational system tends to serve the group rather than the individual. While some blame this on classroom size, we should also revisit our teaching philosophy. Teaching is not a cookie-cutter profession. There is no one right approach for every learner. There is no one right way to teach. The methods and strategies employed by teachers can and should be as varied as the needs of their students.

When a child does not fit the cookie cutter system, we tend to label him or her. What if instead of labeling the more challenging, slower, or disruptive student as learning or behaviorally different, we thought of those students as having *Frizzamyers?* What if we were open to embracing the diversity of our children's God-given design, and gave those differences a universal, non-threatening name? And what if we then looked at those Frizzamyers as qualities that simply required unique solutions?

Currently, our educational system attempts to label and medicate children into submission. Behavioral Frizzamyers are labeled as ADD, ADHD, and a host of other acronyms, and what are considered "appropriate" medications are then prescribed.

But how can a child of two or three or even four truly be diagnosed with a behavioral problem, much less as having a deep-seated psychological imbalance when that child most often cannot even verbally communicate the source of their irritation? And with a child this young, whose emotional, spiritual, and physical well-being rests in the hands of the adults in his world, it only makes sense to look to those *adults* for the source of that child's behavioral anomalies. But instead, we label and medicate.

So what ***is*** a Frizzamyer?

2

ADELOGIC Your Parenting Style

"Soap and education are not as sudden as a massacre, but they are more deadly in the long run."
— Mark Twain, *Sketches New and Old (1900)*

Inventor Thomas Edison's teacher told him he was too stupid to learn anything. Popular wisdom has it that scholar and mathematician Albert Einstein didn't talk until he was about four years old and didn't read until much later. Statesman and Prime Minister Winston Churchill failed sixth grade. Department store founder F. W. Woolworth was told he didn't have common sense. Author Leo Tolstoy flunked out of his university level studies.

What about your son or daughter? Is it conceivable that your child has been mislabeled when, in fact, he or she has been created for splendor? Why are so many young people falling short of their innate greatness? Edison, Einstein, Churchill, Woolworth, Tolstoy—and perhaps your children—have all been victims of labeling.

Edison was probably performing in a way that didn't line up with what his teacher thought should have been the "correct" responses, so he was labeled "stupid." And what do you think Winston Churchill's teachers said when he flunked sixth grade? What did they label him? Lazy? Disinterested?

Today, very young children, unlike the famous people above, are often unable to overcome those labels to achieve the distinction for which they were created. To avoid labeling children in this manner, I coined a word to use instead: "frizzamyer."

A frizzamyer is any unusual way in which a child expresses the existence of an unmet need. When an appropriate need-signaling child behavior, or frizzamyer happens, we can be assured that a child's internal alarm system is working beautifully. Often something needs to be improved during an important stage in their development, so the child acts out to let us know.

By doing away with all the labels and calling these important indicators frizzamyers we take the onus of the behavior off the child and place the responsibility for finding the root cause of it on the adults in his or her environment. Hopefully, this will lead to more desirable outcomes in a child's development.

How Isolation May Have Temporarily Hindered Us

Part of the opportunity created by frizzamyered—mislabeled acting-out kids—is nudging many of us to reevaluate our independent lifestyles. While through the 1960's it was common for people to live within 30 miles of the area in which they grew up, families are now spread out across the country and sometimes the world. With the increase in nuclear families being de-centralized, those members traditionally known for their positive balancing effect—grandparents, aunts, uncles, etc.—have become distanced and even estranged. Now that interrelating between generations is becoming a thing of the past, what is the new American family beginning to look like?

Dr. Bruce Perry calls the effect our society's shift in values has had on our young "marginalizing empathy." With the divorce rate above 50% more and more spouses distance themselves from their former spouses. And with the growth of single-parent families, more parents leave their children in the care of strangers while they go off to work. Children are distanced from their parents as well as from their grandparents, aunts, uncles, cousins, and neighbors, all of whom used to provide our young with their first glimpses of how compassionate people behave. The shock waves from this isolation are now reverberating around the country. And while we would like to believe that quality outsourced child care compensates for all of this, the result of delegating more and more family life to detached professionals is signaling spiritual, intellectual, and emotional destitution in our most vulnerable citizenry, the children.

"The true test of a civilization is, not the census, nor the size of cities—nor the crops—no, but the kind of man the country turns out."
— Emerson, "Civilization," *Society and Solitude* (1870)

The Federal Interagency Forum on Child and Family Statistics tells us that in 2003, some five percent of children ages 4-17 were reported by a parent to have definite or severe difficulties with emotions, concentration, behavior, or being able to get along with other people. Sixty-five percent of the parents of these children reported contacting a mental health professional or general doctor and/or receiving special education for their children to help them. Where do these difficulties come from; what is the source of these frizzamyers? Has anyone asked how many of these children came from isolated family units in which both parents worked? What the family stressors were? Or how often daycare staff were replaced, disinterested in the child/not the teacher's pet, or whether the teacher was in the wrong career to begin with? Statistics like these are alarming enough to encourage further examination.

What we do know is that while parents and children may appear to be alike physically, their most significant resemblances are sometimes overlooked. Children have a compelling desire to model themselves after their most influential relationships. "Like father, like son" is not just an old adage. It is a profound statement of fact. When it comes to finding a hero our little ones first look to us, their parents. And when it comes to their sense of self, we are instrumental in its formation. Thus, when we examine the frizzamyers exhibited by our children, we need also to look to ourselves.

ADELOGIC-a Tool to Help

This book is intended as a tool to help evaluate your family's personal plan for success through a process I call Adelogic. You will discover how to:

- ***ADELOGIC*** your parenting style to get beyond fear and frustration to discovering your child's purpose.
- ***D***ream of what it feels like for your family to win in life - and how to duplicate your success.
- ***E***xplore ways of nurturing your child's ability to rise above inhibitions to a place of empowerment.
- ***L***earn to think beyond the school setting. And consider all of life your ultimate classroom.
- ***O***ccupy your thoughts with the understanding that your child's motivation is more caught than taught.
- ***G***et engaged in what truly inspires you and watch it also inspire your children!
- ***I***gnore obstacles and look for win-win scenarios for your child. Teach them to fail forward.
- ***D***evelop your mastermind team of educators, health care providers and others who will help steer your family's ship into safe harbor. Then fire the rest!

Warning:

My mother played soccer almost up to the day I was born which may account for why my thoughts bounce around from time to time. So please batten down your hatches because this ocean may become a bit unpredictable. May it also be a life changing experience for you!

Most of us enjoy going to an aquatic park to observe trainers getting enormous animals to do amazing things. Perhaps, like me, you have pondered how those guides could have such wonderful, trusting relationships with creatures that could easily annihilate them. It is daunting to conceive the level of patience that both the trainer and the creature must develop to overcome their linguistic and physical differences.

Profound, and at the same time amazingly simple. The instructors do not take away the animals' strength—not even their ability to hurt the trainer. Rather, they empower the creatures to make wise choices that are mutually beneficial. Likewise, I have found that it is entirely possible to discipline children by engaging only their strengths. In the pages of this book, you will learn how I have done this with clients having a wide range of appropriate need-signaling child behaviors, or frizzamyers.

Was Reiner's Preschool For ALL A Modern Day Camelot Story?

The Preschool For All Act (Proposition 82) proposed by Hollywood's Rob Reiner encouraged parents to voluntarily put their young children in preschool. The ad campaigns suggested how much better preschool children did in life. They even said that studies confirmed that kids who went to preschool were more likely to finish college— with no mention of which studies were being referenced or exactly who was included in them. Hmm! We were encouraged to join in taking money from the rich to help the poor and needy. That no holds barred campaign certainly seemed to have a lot of us scrambling to do the right thing. While this was one theory, there is another set of data that I find even more compelling.

> *"People do not do a thing because it's right; they do a thing because they feel it's right."*
> — Zig Ziglar

In the summer of 2005, the Child Care and Development Planning Council's Early Childhood Mental Health Subcommittee heard a proposal on the expulsion rates of children in state and other publicly funded preschools. As stated, preschool children are being expelled from childcare settings at a rate that is 3 times greater than those being kicked out of K-12. Obviously preschool and K-12 are separate entities, but could you have imagined that those entering a school setting for the very first time would be at the center of a nationwide epidemic far greater than those in K-12? There has even been a campaign to seek legislation that would require classes on "challenging behavior" in addition to the regular program and curriculum courses for early childhood educators. Yet it is my observation that expulsion often results despite appropriate need-signaling child behaviors, or frizzamyers. Proponents of universal preschool have developed such strikingly similar initiatives for impacting "every" young child in America that the question becomes: how have they completely missed the nationwide preschool expulsion epidemic? How do we get educators to recognize these frizzamyers as the child's call for assistance, as a signal of a need not being met or a part of their life that is not conducive to healthy growth, an invaluable form of communication? How do we equip educators to translate that communication? And to deal with it in a way conducive to the healthy emotional, social, spiritual, and intellectual development of the child? And how do universal preschool advocates see a "state" or national institution reversing all this without even the slightest mention of it?

What has happened to the notion of school readiness? Could it be that the supposed "misbehavior" and the resulting expulsion comes about because we have evolved to the place where this many little ones now have mental illness in America? Or is the preponderance of Frizzamyers a signal that our preschool system and expectations, as well as our family infrastructures, are failing to meet the needs of the children they serve?

A New Paradigm to Consider

Nearly all of the current models for addressing the very special needs of children and their families (including behavior modification, parenting classes, and prescription drugs to control behavior problems) are often based on preconceived notions about the young. Generalizations are often used to affirm a one-size-fits-all model drawn solely from a child's observable behavior. Some of this conduct is labeled attention deficit hyperactivity disorder (ADHD), oppositional defiance (OD), the whole autism spectrum, along with a number of other labels that have been applied to small children. While some diagnoses may be valid, the vast number of children "diagnosed" belies the validity of the majority and instead suggests a dearth of knowledge and patience with which to address the individual needs of our children.

My role as a Pre-school and Family Life Coach is to create a safe environment in which a family experiences their own self-discovery. My life coaching practice has not drawn its answers from celebrities, politicians or medical mandates, but rather from listening to and interacting with families. I have found that frizzamyers being played out in a child's life are indicating something much deeper. The child who regularly displays a frizzamyer is shouting that he or she has an inner need still waiting to be met. Our job as parents is often to become private investigators in search of the root cause, and then in helping restore our children's sense of balance.

There are cases in which we are predisposed to doing so. If a child becomes withdrawn, starts wetting the bed, and becomes depressed, then educators, physicians, and even parents tend to look for some identifiable state of disease, for something in the child's environment engendering these behaviors. It has become a part of our consciousness to describe these combined frizzamyers as they relate to antecedents. But what might these or any other combinations of frizzamyers signal? Why haven't we looked further? And how do we separate our regard for the child from the impact of his or her behavior so that we can dispassionately assess the root of the frizzamyer without blaming the child.

With this in mind, the table on the following page compares the current medical model of behavior management/modification and my approach to un-labeling child behavior,.

The Medical Model	ADELOGIC Model
Prolonged inappropriate child behavior dictates pharmaceutical intervention.	Child responses to life are adapted to circumstances as the child views them.
The severity of the behavior drives the medications and/or therapy for the child.	Severe behaviors provide the best indicators of the child's underlying need.
Clinicians serve as the experts or authorities over the course of action.	*Pre-school and Family Life Coaching* operates as a subordinate partner in the family's alliance with the parents as the final authorities.
Treatment is focused primarily on short-term solutions based on the child's past.	Coaching is focused primarily on the long-term potential for empowering the child.
The compulsory approach ignores both the physical and emotional impact on the child.	This parent-driven alliance honors the well-being of the family and the child.
The child is the one needing altering.	The child is *never* the problem!
The child is viewed in fragments based on whose lens is used, i.e. psychiatrist, school psychologist, teacher…	The child remains a whole person where family, community, education, food, and chemicals all impact their behavior.

All children are created for greatness. Recently, following a presentation that I gave, a couple sought my services. The mother was grieving as she told me of her children's long-standing struggles in school. It seemed that their teachers were persuaded that the children needed a great deal more discipline in their study habits and social interactions if they were ever to become fully capable learners.

Once Mom sensed that her true feelings were safe, she confided in me that the children had recently been adopted. She then began to tell me about the tremendous hurdles that her family had overcome in their ordeal.

However, as I began to coach them, a light suddenly came on for this couple. She and her husband together began to see that they needed less emphasis on academics at that junction in their children's development, and more on ensuring that their children felt safe and secure in their new family. They came to realize that it would take time for their children to adjust and accept the permanence of their new situation and that it was important to work on this construct while simultaneously supporting their children's academic performance.

Together, this couple determined to explore their own lead, following their instincts in understanding what their children's frizzamyers were indicating. Thank God for fearless parents like these who are strong enough to think outside the box despite pressure from the outside!

Parenting is seldom easy. Like any skill, the art of parenting without fear is an acquired one. And parents make mistakes. But it is the acceptance of parenting as a training ground where new skills are continually being honed that makes strong parents—and that provides our children with the best opportunity to fully develop their potential.

Are you ready to start your journey toward discovering the wonder and awe of the little ones in your life?

3

Create and Sustain a Strong Family

Once upon a time, some animals decided they must do something heroic to meet the problems of a new world, so they organized a school. They adopted an activity curriculum consisting of running, climbing, swimming and flying. To make the program easier to administer, all the animals took all of the subjects.

The duck was superb at swimming, better in fact than his instructor, and made excellent grades in flying, but he was very poor in running. Since he was low in running skills, he had to stay after school, drop swimming, and practice running. He kept this up until his webbed feet were badly worn, and he was only average in swimming. But average was acceptable in this school, so nobody worried about it, except the duck.

The rabbit started at the top of the class in running, but had a nervous breakdown because of so much makeup in swimming.

The squirrel was excellent in climbing until he developed frustrations in the flying class where his teacher made him start from the ground and fly up instead of coming down from the tree-top. He also developed leg cramps from overexertion. He got a C in climbing and a D in running.

The eagle was a problem child and had to be disciplined severely. In climbing class he beat all the others to the top of the tree, but insisted on using his own way of getting there.

At the end of the year, an abnormal eel that could swim exceedingly well and also could run, climb, and fly a little had the highest average and was valedictorian.

The prairie dogs stayed out of school and fought the tax levy because the administration would not add digging and burrowing to the curriculum. They apprenticed their children to the badger and later joined the groundhogs and gophers to start a successful private school.

> *"Train up a child in the way he should go,*
> *Even when he is old he will not depart from it."*
> — King Solomon et al, Proverbs 22:6
> (OEM or Original Equipment
> Manufacturer's Handbook)

So How Was School Today?

Dr. Reeves' story about a group of animals in a standardized classroom environment teaches us what can happen when a curriculum is imposed on children to make it easier to administer, all at the expense of their God-given gifts and abilities. I challenge you to get past the word "free" and start focusing on the fine print before signing your child over to the state. In the end, convenience may exact a higher price than you will be able to repay.

During my college internship with the County Child Care Coordinator's office (a department that has since been dissolved) I found myself on the inside of many childcare programs. I even did some advocacy work at the state level in Sacramento, California. Now that I am in my forties and the mother of a young child, I am taking a fresh look at educational systems and learning approaches. This time, I'm looking with greater intensity because the well-being of my own child may be at stake.

To this end, I have established an innovative model of restoring wellness, known as the "Fearless Parenting Institute LLC." This pre-school and family life coaching approach is based on the principle that while the child's frizzamyers may be problematic, the child is not the problem. I have found that having this belief system makes it much easier to focus on what is actually disturbing a little one's peace of mind.

It is understood in the Fearless Parenting Institute LLC that the existence of a special need in a child is far from being a setback. It is the outward display of an appropriate need-signaling child behavior, or frizzamyer. Pre-school and family life coaching responds to a younger client's exclamation by helping the family identify the area of their environment that is causing the imbalance. As a result of this approach, many of my real world clients have been transitioned right out of special education, and even out of residential treatment altogether. That is not to say that there are not children with severe learning disabilities who do have their own brand of special needs. However, what we are addressing here is the frizzamyered child misdiagnosed as a special needs student.

Sneaking in the Back Door

Contrary to the preschool posts on current campaign websites, however, there are, unquestionably, many worthwhile early childhood settings in operation. However, according to the body of research that I have reviewed, they do not make up the majority. Therefore my approach to getting a good look at today's preschool programs is to be as inconspicuous as possible. I have found that calling the director of a school and asking for a tour has not proven to be sufficient because, as might be expected, everybody is on his or her best behavior. Instead, I prefer to show up at childcare facilities entirely unannounced. Time and again, I have been amazed at how much more information I obtain this way.

One day while still a newborn, Dree needed a break from riding in the car, as well as a good burp session. So I stopped at a fully-accredited and licensed childcare center (supposedly a "very reputable" facility) and parked under a shade tree near the play area.

What timing! Just then, an employee was bringing the babies into the yard. What initially caught my eye as a former preschool director was the interaction of one staff member with a child. As I watched I was struck by the manner in which the employee grabbed the child off the ground and then firmly slammed him back down again. Now that they had my rapt and shocked attention, I settled in for at least an hour of observation.

Surely, I thought, this was just a fluke! Perhaps this adult was having a bad day. I tried desperately to quell the anger that was welling up inside me.

Soon, these babies were replaced on the playground by six of their toddler peers and a different staff member. This time, I expected to see something that would warm my heart. I thought I would see an approved institutional childcare facility providing the optimal environment for school readiness.

Immediately after the children arrived on the scene, I saw that their only caregiver's attention was somewhere else instead of being on those in her charge. I kept watching for another caregiver to come out to the playground who would engage these anxious little ones in outdoor activities. But it didn't happen. So I started looking in the same direction that the lone staff person was staring.

In a few minutes, another child was brought to her, increasing the ratio of one caregiver to seven barely walking preschool children. Young ones thrive having a great deal of one-on-one attention, so I wondered how excellence could be provided to this many children by one caregiver whose attention was obviously elsewhere.

To make matters worse, the child diverting the caregiver's attention apparently belonged to her. Evidently, playground time was when the caregiver gave herself to her mother-child relationship. I had to ask myself, Would I be willing to pay a program staff member to nurture her own child while ignoring mine? Oh yes, this staff member did include the other children by introducing them to her son. As children will, these young ones surrounded the worker, so much so that as she moved around the yard with her son, the other children tagged along.

Admittedly, that got my frizzamyers into a bundle. Perhaps my standards are outdated, but I had hoped to see some connection between each child and a staff member. Perhaps the interface might have included a hug, tying a shoe, reading a book, or just looking at the trees together. Instead, when one of the children experienced conflict, this "caregiver" spoke to him from a distance while standing fully erect.

Her posture struck me as peculiar, because to a young child adults can seem huge, and in stressful situations they can even resemble giants. Simply bending down and drawing the little one close while speaking softly to him might have been enough to calm his fears. But in this case, partly because of the remoteness of the caregiver, the child continued his frizzamyer for quite some time and through many tears. I suspected that I might only have been seeing the tip of the iceberg of problems in this childcare center.

I held my Dree a little bit closer and was reminded how privileged children are when, as fearless parents, we place them among our highest priorities.

These Children Will Conform!

While there is no doubt that children thrive best in a loving, consistent family environment, as discussed earlier, there is also no doubt that in today's world it is not always preferable for a parent or even a member of the extended family to be the primary caregiver. Thus the need for extraordinary vigilance in choosing an alternative caretaker whose values and method of childcare closely resemble those of the child's family.

Also please understand that while this book starts with and focuses on preschool—because that is where our children begin their relationship with the formal educational system—I am a preschool and family life coach, and to that end, when I began my practice, I supported families with children of all ages, on a select basis.

Treatment team meetings are part of the collaborative service that my practice provides. Here is an example of an encounter that further illustrates the need for a family-driven paradigm for children.

Gathered around a table was the mom, a service coordinator with the agency that was paying my tab, our client's special education teacher, a licensed clinical therapist—all members of the treatment team—and myself. Because of the strides our client had made in a very short period of time through my practice, we were discussing the option of ending services.

During the discussion, we remarked that within just a few months of coaching, this client had greatly improved her attentiveness, positive response to critical feedback, AWOL (running away from school) behavior, enuresis (urinating on herself) and a plethora of other frizzamyers. Prior to this, the licensed therapist had been meeting on a daily basis with the client child in her school setting for about a year without any sustained improvement. It was the opinion of both the mother and myself that the original reasons for my services no longer existed.

The clinician suggested that we needed to continue the coaching alliance. The coordinator then asked the clinician to explain the medical necessity for continuing pre-school and family life coaching for this public school student. The clinician then turned to me for the response.

I told her that my practice was not clinical and that I did not make such decisions for my families, but that they determine how long my services were required in meeting their needs. The clinician did not approve of this answer. So she repeated her question for me. I told her that families determined when they wanted coaching, how often they wanted to be coached, and how they should be coached. The clinician became visibly flustered and exclaimed, "Well, this is certainly not conventional protocol!"

"Do a common thing in an uncommon way."
— Booker T. Washington

The coordinator then got into a discourse about what the clinician was actually doing to facilitate the child's stabilization. The clinician said that she had developed a contract between the child and the teacher. In an effort to learn the inner-workings of this contract, I asked the clinician how it was being implemented. She said that it stated that this child "will not disrupt the classroom and will not put their hands on others." The clinician had them agree to this arrangement. The teacher said that when the child did a good job, she earned points. When she did not finish a task, she was required to make it up during recess.

Hint:
The will is most resilient in the face of challenges, and can withstand some of the most crushing assaults.

By contrast, our spirit is as delicate as a rose and can be temporarily crushed if trampled on enough times with the right amount of emotional force.

I took special note that after a year of the teacher and the clinician rehearsing their choice of anti-team building language, their collective contract concept continued to work with minimal success at best. The reason their idea was not working effectively was because the child's will was being impacted much more by the contract than her spirit. She took on this daily contract in a way similar to what one would do with a sparring partner. And guess who seemed to be winning?

Even though the experts were consistently upholding their professionally-powered agreement, the child was experiencing it as negative reinforcement. What she needed in order to be a thriving young student was being overlooked. The child firmly resisted the experts in this case because she had not been included in deciding her own success in the classroom, a task for which she was fully qualified. Although it appears that those in charge missed that critical point, our client didn't.

The teacher then asked how I would go about getting a better response from our client. I said that it was all about her empowerment. She was an articulate student, so I would ask her how she, if given the choice, would like to spend her recess. Once she told me, I would then fully encourage her in her desire and even offer to add intrigue to the activity in some way. For example, I might tell her that finishing her assignment would afford her the very privilege she hoped for. The choice would be entirely hers to make. I told the teacher that I believed a greater measure of success in this situation could be achieved by including the child in the decision-making process and emphasizing her opportunity and self-determination.

Almost every situation in childhood,
if viewed as a teachable moment,
can result in life skills learned.
— Adelaide Zindler, FP

I had coached this child to develop the kind of critical thinking that both she and I would expect from leaders-in-training. As a result, she began mainstreaming right out of special education classes. Because of her miraculous turnaround, she and I were interviewed by Lisa Lake from Channel 10 in San Diego, California.

When a child is misunderstood and nothing is done to remedy the situation, his or her spirit can be wounded. When this occurs, some children will escalate their behaviors, while others will retreat within themselves. In either case, for the actions I identify as frizzamyers, children are labeled and even medicated while the original problem remains unresolved. Prescriptions and therapies may stave off conflict for a while—but only when they are working; they are a panacea, not a cure!

Finding Purpose Begins With Tiny Steps

After graduating from college, one of my first assignments was as a substitute teacher in the public school system. There, I was afforded the privilege of learning from kindergarteners, twelfth graders, and many students in grades in between. What stood out to me from these experiences was how influential we adults are to children.

I entered one primary level special education classroom in which a teacher's aide took me aside and informed me that one student in particular would not be a problem for me as the aide had been instructed to work with the student that day. I told the aide that in that case we would be switching roles so she could enjoy a break from the routine. She could assist the others for a change, and I would focus on this student's needs on a one-on-basis. The aide seemed taken off guard by my directive.

When we gathered around the table to trace letters, the child, in perfect Pavlovian style, became frustrated and began banging his head on the table and hitting his head with his hands. The aide stared at the child and me in apparent condescension. But I tried to look at the world through the child's eyes. I told him that he was capable of doing anything he saw the other students doing. He insisted that I was mistaken, so I offered to prove my point. Now that I had his attention, I put a fat pencil in his hand, held my hand over his, and together we began to slowly form the letters. If only you could have seen the look on his face! No professional actor could have portrayed the same smile his face depicted—the sheer bliss of an accomplishment that literally took his breath away. I eased my grip as subtly as I could until he began to work alongside his peers.

"There ain't no rules around here.
We're trying to accomplish something."
— Thomas Edison, Inventor

During lunch and again at recess, I received many stares from staff members who, in keeping with some strange custom, isolated themselves from the students. I found this to be the case in most all of the free public schools in which I was assigned. I also noticed that there were mounds of accumulated trash in the children's play area. The custodial team was apparently not assigned to patrol this area of campus, so I organized the students in a race to see who could collect the most garbage by the end of recess. Together, we cleaned the yard and ended recess with a hug.

Now let's see—what did we accomplish? What about dynamic social interaction, environmental awareness, physical exercise, and life invigorating human touch as the reward for a job well done? How was that for emergent curriculum arising out of the circumstances?

I read through the laundry list of instructions left by the teacher for whom I was substituting. The teacher's emphasis for that day was on teaching the children to count. Since this was a combination first and second grade class, I decided to convert the written assignment into a kinesthetic (hands-on) model.

One of my special needs is to be without shoes whenever possible. And would you believe that the children were willing to accommodate me by taking theirs off too? We created a human circle and began the lesson by counting each wiggling toe. Expanding on this successful strategy, we began with our lower multiplication tables.

You would not believe how much easier multiplication was for the children when they were able to use their hands and feet instead of just memorizing the information in their heads! Or how quickly they grasped the concept! In fact, I couldn't tell who the most gifted children were, because everyone was shouting out the right answers and not merely "guestimates" which had become so popular in public schools. The day seemed to fly by. I was in awe that these little geniuses let me spend time in their presence.

A Case Study

There are so many stories, but I'll just tell one more. This time, I was in a senior high school special education class—although it seemed more like a funeral hall where I had come to pay my last respects. No one seemed to notice that I had even entered the room. Some boys were playing a video game called Cops and Crops. They told me that it was a game about stealing drugs and evading the authorities. I learned from the teacher's assistant that this "curriculum" had been approved for purchase by the school's administration, rather than by the students. Hmm...

Some girls were talking among themselves. Staff members were huddled in a separate corner of the room doing the same. Other students simply stared at the blank walls. One of them, who seemed quite studious for this group, was engrossed in math problems. He was using a calculator to compute simple addition.

When I introduced myself to the students and asked about the thick atmosphere in the classroom, I was soon told that nobody cared about them, which was why they were all in this class in the first place. There was seemingly no goal for them being at school. In fact, it seemed as if they felt that there was little or no purpose for them at all!

Stop the press! Say what? To me, this was unacceptable. These children were there to be nurtured. Those of us mandated with their care were there to help them reach their physical, intellectual, spiritual and even emotional potential. Instead, they had been made to feel like cast-offs. Something needed to be done.

I can't say whether or not we turned the world on its heels that day. But during a break, not only did I share my testimony to encourage their hearts, I went home and emptied my refrigerator of every single vegetable. I then hauled my very heavy juicer all the way back to the school, and gave them an impromptu introduction in nutrition. Because the classroom was completely devoid of age-appropriate stimulation, I needed something to do with my hands and something for the student's to do with theirs. So we started juicing. I even got a mean-faced foster child to squeeze some juice. You'd have thought I had asked him to climb Mount Everest in his bare feet! The juicing exercise engaged them, and once engaged, like any children these children were more open to all kinds of instruction. The calculator king learned that his brain could run rings around that little machine.

Consider just a few of their special needs. One young man was an accomplished welder. He worked every day after he got out of school to help make ends meet for his family. Another young lady was frustrated that her mother's significant other was enjoying more than his share of the amenities—including the younger siblings. He played the pedophile, while she assumed the role of Mom after school. Real special needs indeed!

While educators are now being told to stay away from the personal with the children in their charge, how can we educate unless we do so holistically? In particular, how can we meet the needs of so-called special-needs children without knowing the dynamics that create their frizzamyers.

Children are people with needs, wants, hopes, dreams, and feelings. They feel pressure to perform. They react and respond to positive and negative feedback. Their emotions can be as varied and complex as those of any adult, and the stressors they face are often experienced at far greater levels of intensity. Each child is born with potential, but life experiences often get in the way of them exercising that potential; promising hopefuls often become caught in the crossfire of adverse environmental input. It is up to every adult caretaker to assess those blockages and see to it that our children have the opportunity to maximize their intellectual, spiritual, emotional, and physical potential. That can only be done through a truly caring and holistic approach where fearless parents lead the way!

"Every child is an artist. The problem is how to remain an artist once he grows up."
— Pablo Picasso

In Search of Your Child's Purpose

Older generations have challenged us to invest in our children regardless of what may be required. Tim Kimmel, PhD, takes it to the next level in his book *Grace-Based Parenting* by shocking readers with his uncanny view of what childrearing ought to be about:

> *We need to have kids that can be sent off to the most hostile universities, toil in the greediest work environments, and raise their families in the most hedonistic communities and yet not be the least bit intimidated by their surroundings. Furthermore, they need to be engaged in the lives of people in their culture, gracefully representing Christ's love inside these desperate surroundings.*

I cited Dr. Kimmel's book so often that my best friend brought it to her women's group, and they turned it into a study. I was overjoyed with what came out of their support group, but not nearly as much as their children were, I'm sure.

God has a purpose for every life, and it is our job as parents, teachers, coaches, rabbis, pastors, and even pediatricians to help the children in our care find it. After all, who knows what unique contribution that seemingly difficult child has to offer our society?

By the way, has your sense of fearlessness begun to awaken?

4

Empower Your Child Beyond Inhibitions

"Empowerment" is a word that gets used a lot these days. Increasingly, big corporations such as Petco and others are retaining life-coaching services to empower their teams to win big. In so doing, they are seeing more of their employees take control of their own ventures within the company. Staff are also becoming more responsible for the quality of their work and benefiting from the rewards that follow. This investment on the part of employers doesn't just benefit the employees. It also is of benefit to the customers as well as the interests of the overall corporation. The members of an organization and its employees, are part of the team. Coaching helps the team work better both individually and as a unit, thus inspiring innovation and overall productivity.

In the interest of the education of our children, let's look at a forward-thinking business model. Logan and King, authors of *The Coaching Revolution*, remind us that the business world now operates on Internet time. To be at their most productive, employees need coaching and not constraint. Why would children be an exception to this rule? Logan and King further believe that in the workplace, billions are being squandered in the way of human potential. The same can be said of the upcoming generation as well. Where long term forward momentum is favored, they argue that few if any changes result from formal group training. The content is pre-approved and the level of risk minimal. It's cheap and easy to come by. How are preschools different? Preschools generally allow as many as 20 children in one walled-in room with the faculty/student ratio at sub-optimum. When the teacher student ratio is optimal, the learning curve is shortened. When coaching is one on one, it is at it's best!

The Fearless Parenting Institute LLC is the first to specialize in offering similar tools to families of young children. Consider each family as a team whose members each bring strengths to the group that make it function better as a whole. How do we keep that team working well together while nurturing all its members? How does the leader maximize their potential, and at the same time empower each member of the team?

Parents often feel adrift in a sea of responsibilities and compromises. In order to meet the financial responsibilities of their families, they are forced to compromise functionality. And when assistance is needed, particularly in getting their family back on track, they see it as a sign of weakness, of embarrassment. But a bit of coaching can do wonders for getting a family life back in balance.

Nearly all of the athletic champions you can think of have required coaching to get there. By holding a coaching lantern high enough above their circumstance, families are able to see their opportunity to function more consistently with their ideals, and to see their goals solidly within reach. At this point, by using the accountability that coaching is known for, they can be easily empowered to initiate the steps required to effect the life they've only dreamed possible. Explore this further in the *Fearless Parenting Audio Training* Series available only at www.fearlessparenting.com.

During a corporate coaching session this was certainly made clear to my clients. What started out as a seemingly trivial discussion about how to implement a new proposal quickly took a different turn. Picking up on sub-surface tension between co-workers who seemed to be on opposite sides of the fence, I asked permission to take a detour from the agenda. I saw that clearing the air might restore the focus necessary in furthering their discussion that morning. Because I had their trust, they were eager for any input I could give. It seemed that this was not the first time emotions had flared up.

After setting a tone of emotional safety within the group I operated as their facilitator and became responsible for guiding their interaction peacefully. In less than an hour we were able to learn that the need to be respected was at the root of the problem. One older team member from a different ethnic background struggled with the attitude of a much younger team player who had a seemingly arrogant communication style. While the older member felt certain he was being singled out for no apparent reason, neither had considered that they shared similar misconceptions about each other. Together they agreed upon very specific steps that they would take to overcome their challenges with each other in the interest of the project. It was an eye opener for them and a lesson that whole team benefited from participating in. One of the keys to this successful outcome is that it was not a part of a designated training session, but rather it naturally surfaced during a routine business planning meeting. Only this time coaching created a safe space for communication and for the healing process to begin. Most training does not result in behavioral change. One-on-one coaching knocks years off the time it normally takes us to create champions in the corporate and in the family culture as well.

Empowerment for All

Let's consider a formal definition of the word "empowerment." One meaning refers to increasing the strength of individuals. Empowerment can also mean imparting a decision-making process to those who have previously been denied such access. It involves endowing a person with confidence that he or she is an invaluable contributor to society.

Can you imagine an America in which our most vulnerable members were given this gift from the start? Miraculously we empower our youngest family members when Daddy speaks to his baby in the womb, and Mom bounces her unborn while moving to the rhythm of her favorite song. However, similar to the interdependence they experience in utero, many children also thrive when given options in their new world. This can be initiated with meal preparation, simple clothing decisions, and even selecting a family activity.

Participating in the decision-making process not only makes children feel like substantial members of the family team, it also prepares them for making crucial decisions later in life. Some parents have developed the habit of including their children in helping plan the family schedule, thus turning a once routine experience into an adventure that extends to their mealtimes, vacations, bedtime rituals, and even conflict resolution. Even managing wealth can then become a natural outgrowth of such an informal learning structure. But most importantly, including our children in the decision-making process within the family empowers them to make healthier decisions when faced with peer pressure later on.

Empowerment on the Home Front

Did you know that "housekeeper" once meant property owner, and "infant" meant anyone under 21 years of age?

Sometimes it is the gift of time that helps us best navigate the often turbulent waters of parenting.

Our daughter Dree is entering her preschool years. Periodically, she demonstrates her willingness to stand her ground at all costs. A while back she kicked things up a notch, and as a result I had to dismiss any pattern I might have seen in how she responds to discipline. The lesson we'd been working on was putting our things away when we finished with them. She'd seen my own example of this throughout the day. We even had a song that we rocked out to while we picked up the room. However, she recently made me realize that I needed to be more consistent in supporting her in following through.

This particular morning, I encouraged Dree to put her toys away before breakfast. Demonstrating how well she understood what she was asked to do, she put away one of the dishes that she had been using, leaving at least six other items where she had played with them. Initially it might sound like food was being withheld as a form of discipline, which I would not endorse. Had this scenario continued into lunchtime or even been beyond my foreknowledge of my child's strong willed nature for that matter, I would certainly have altered the discipline accordingly.

Because I had given her a heads up in plenty of time, when I noticed that she was "stiffening her neck," so to speak, I told her that when she was ready to complete her assigned task, her breakfast would be waiting for her. I then ate without her.

Dree started screaming and then came over to me, seemingly in shock that I would make such a big deal out of this. I simply encouraged her to put her toys away so that she could have breakfast.

She dropped to the floor in melodramatic flare and began bawling with "tears as big as a horse's," as my husband would say. To see the way she carried on, you'd have thought for sure that I was abusing her. And although I know better, seeing her cry almost weakened my resolve!

However, with her best interests and long-term development in mind, I calmly reminded Dree of the original plan. I even brought her over to the floor where the toys still remained to remind her of how we do things. Yet nothing was going to persuade her on this morning. Dree would simply not pick up the other items. That's when I decided to get on the computer and start re-editing this chapter. She tagged along behind me, screaming all the way.

By this time, breakfast had long been over and my ever-determined daughter remained unwavering in her decision to stand her ground against cleanup time. So I decided to go and pick a piece of fruit from the tree outside. I showed it to her, and immediately she reached for it. I then reminded her again that as soon as she cleaned up her area, the delicacy would be hers along with the rest of breakfast.

Firm in her decision, Dree curled up and fell asleep from sheer exhaustion as I typed the manuscript for this book. As her mother, this was so difficult for me. For at least 2 hours—if not more—I had walked over with her to that same spot where the toys were, but to no avail, exhausting both her and me in the process. However, by 11:00 a.m., she was finally ready to give in. When we approached the assignment this time, Dree decided to pick up all of her toys as I had asked. She went so far as to pick up everything around her, and even looked for more to clean. After this eternity in a child's sense of time, Dree finally chose to respond with obedience.

As a reader, your reaction to this might be, "I don't have this kind of time." But time spent like this during your child's developmental years means far less of your time might have to be spent cajoling and coercing in the future, while simultaneously providing your child with security borne of your consistency. These are the interactions that set the tone of your relationship with your child; while frustrating, they are a necessary component to defining your role and his. Investing at the level of your child's need early on, though momentarily constraining, can make future parenting challenges far less difficult.

My takeaways from this exercise were numerous. The lesson engaged her will but never bruised her spirit, as evidenced by her joyful disposition each time we walked back to the "crime scene." As I sat beside her while she finally ate her meal, we shared warm facial expressions and an endearing mother/daughter conversation. Dree did not place her challenge on my shoulders by staying angry with me, but clearly decided the outcome for herself.

Believing that I could guide my child without using negative reinforcement, I merely served as her facilitator, speaking to her in soft and loving tones. I made sure that I encouraged her to do what needed to be done, while restraining from making this my own personal issue. She held the controls throughout the ordeal, steering the outcomes on her own terms because of the precious gift of unhurried time.

Often, as parents we give in well before our children would have. By allowing Dree the freedom she needed to master this important lesson, I sensed her beginning to establish a pattern of perseverance that she'll need later in her life. Despite her age, her uncanny ability to stay the course was fully utilized in guiding her toward an optimal choice.

The immediate return on my investment with Dree is evident in how well she is known to handle herself in public most of the time. If I think about what I want for her future, the fleeting time I spend in deve-loping her character now will very likely pay huge dividends for many years to come.

Just to keep me on my toes, this experience taught her to dig her heels into the ground even harder against putting her things away the next time. So once I got over it being a personal attack on me I adapted my approach to the change in my little scientist. I am careful to nurture cleanliness after each activity rather than only certain ones. No sleeping on this job folks! As I continue to watch her grow, I am thrilled at allowing her the time she needs to find her way. We have far fewer conflicts than would ever constitute "the terrible twos." Even though she continues to test her boundaries, she responds well when her parents reinforce them, remembering that we will hold the boundaries with steady hands regardless of which way she needs to squirm within them.

"I had... found that motherhood was a profession by itself, just like school teaching and lecturing."
— Ida B. Wells

Considering Your Own Core Values

As a parent, consistency is one of your most potent tools. Given positive consistency, predictable responses, a child may still push the boundaries, but he or she will thrive. There is reassurance in bumping a boundary and not having it move, and in parents being predictable in their responses. Consistency breeds security, and secure children are better able to handle the stressors the world throws at them.

On a radio show, a well-respected chaplain once told the audience of his experience. He was often asked to give last rites at the deathbed of multi-millionaires in America. He said that he had never heard them regret not making that last deal, or of leaving unfinished business at the office. Instead, they often were grief-stricken that they had sacrificed time with their families in favor of work. The chaplain heard this theme repeated time after time among our nation's most well to do.

How wealth and its accumulation is approached influences a family for generations. Have you considered how your core beliefs about material resources impact the amount of time you spend on the business of family building? Or how your values influence your children's self-image? Making wise decisions is a responsibility of affluence—one that rewards us, our families, and those who are influenced by us.

What would others learn about you if they looked at your checkbook register? In his book *When God Whispers Your Name*, Max Lucado tells of a nationwide study of our American values. Tragically, here's what that study found. For $10,000,000:

- 25% of us would leave our families
- 23% of us would engage in prostitution for a
- few days
- 16% of us would give away our birthright as
- Americans
- 16% of us would leave our marriages
- 13% of us would give our children away

So what are your life and family worth? Have you ever pondered what your days will be like when your time on Earth is at its end? How do you want to be remembered and what will be your legacy? We would do well to ask ourselves such questions because they can be critical in restoring balance in our family's lives.

If you've been looking for a table topic, consider a family discussion around these same questions. You might find them to be wonderful ways of determining if the life you have chosen has met your own expectations-not to mention the return your Creator is expecting from His investment in you. What it comes down to is the age-old question: What do you want on your dash?

"Good thinkers are always in demand.
A person who knows how, may always have a job,
but the person who knows why will always
be his boss."
— John Maxwell in *Thinking for a Change*

Real World Decisions

We live in the richest country on earth, and our expectations have come to reflect this. Middle class has grown to mean a four-bedroom, two-and-a-half bath home in a good neighborhood. Most of us expect our children to go to college, to be professionals. While these goals are laudable, there is a downside to our upwardly mobile attitude.

We possess multiple televisions, stereos, and cars. We go on wonderful vacations. But we are so busy with the work it takes to acquire all these material possessions and with the activities in which we have involved our children that we seldom have time for dinner together. We have so much technological input that we rarely converse as a family. But some of us are beginning to reprioritize.

We are seeing the need to separate basic living requirements from wants. To consider our needs as individuals, as family members, and as members of a macro society. And we are enjoining our loved ones in this process.

For example, think about how your family has chosen to take action in response to the cost of gasoline and heating oil. Has the cost of petroleum or the glut of U.S. foreclosures impacted your finances? What actions are you taking microcosmically and macrocosmically? How are you tightening your belts as a family, and what are you doing to reverse the crisis that threatens your ability to remain free? Or are you just hoping the government will find a way to bring the price back down?

As parents, we know instinctually what is right for our families, and yet we have been ceding more and more of the decision-making power to the government at greater and greater costs, both emotional and financial. Here's a whopper of an example for you! Ever wonder what $9.4 billion of our tax dollars would get us? The findings from Investing in Quality: A Survey of State Child Care and Development Fund Initiatives, April 2006, put out by the National Association of State Child Care Administrators (NASCCA) Child Trends, and the Bank Street College of Education, at a cost of $9.4 billion, answers the question for us. So what did they give us for our hard earned tax dollars? The bottom line as I read it is that they then needed another opportunity to "strengthen the capacity for evaluation" because they didn't quite get there on that dime. Can't you just hear a plea for another one of these pricey little initiatives?

However, I was most attracted to what they did find to be of value. The goal of those billions was to urge low income families to place their young children in institutional childcare and find work. While it seemed politically correct to focus on social and emotional well-being in the programs, a large majority of that money was split between health and safety (23%) and administration (23%). In fact above all else health and safety was the weakest area overall. Since these programs can't even begin to address higher level thinking skills until they have made their facilities physically safe for children, no wonder they haven't gotten off the bench. Aside from this, family related matters got a whole 6% of the budget, while the actual children got 0%. Wow! I wonder what would have resulted had these agencies asked families what they needed in order to succeed, then put some resources toward their goals?

When it comes down to it, families are responsible for themselves and their children. With all the best of intentions, the government is an institution, and institutions are not families. We need to reprioritize so that we become our children's bulwark.

With fewer of these high-end studies, we might be able to retire our national debt. Now that's what I'd call a true Camelot remake!

Loved, nurtured, disciplined, and made to feel part of a family, there is no limit to what our children can achieve. As the story goes, Philo Farnsworth's parents originally anticipated him becoming a concert violinist. When he was 12 years old he built a motor and his family's first washing machine. He discovered the concept of television as a boy, and reportedly transmitted his very first image at 21 years of age. And all that from having to find something to do around the house? Did he ever become a concert violinist? Does it matter?

*"There's nothing on it worthwhile,
and we're not going to watch it in this household,
and I don't want it in your intellectual diet."*
— Philo Farnsworth

So if you find your family wanting to pull away from one of your favorite T.V. shows to participate in our Club Fearless Newsletter, or Blog, you can take confidence that its inventor would applaud you thrill seekers. I sure hope you'll join us too!

Sharpening Your Child's Wealth Management Skills

As opposed to positive stress, negative stress almost always has a harmful impact on families, and with most American families at least one salary year in debt, financial stress is at an all-time high. In our more-is-better buy-it-on-credit society, how do we reign ourselves in? When children's birthday parties have taken on social significance way beyond the celebration of a special day to become proving grounds for our financial wherewithal, how do we keep from overspending? When we are judged for our material possessions as much or more than for our character, how do we restore our reputation? When our children's friends have unlimited credit cards, how do we hold to a reasonable approach to allowance and spending?

And amidst all this, how do we impart good financial values to our children?

Who taught you the skills you use in making important decisions? Have your children learned to value others, themselves and their money from watching you? What is the right age to begin actively developing these skills in them?

My husband and I were not financially savvy when we came into our marriage. I regularly overindulged and thoroughly enjoyed spending our resources, while my husband routinely bailed me out. *Working Woman Magazine* even featured my story. However, some years ago, I found a substantial opportunity to establish longer-term rewards. It was then that this whole quest to give children financial training wheels became of critical importance to me. I was introduced to the book *Faith and Finance* by Dr. Timothy J. Winters, and found it to be a wonderful resource for jumpstarting my journey. Here are a few excerpts from his book:

> Like Grape Nuts cereal. They're not grapes and neither are they nuts. The same is true about "good credit." Credit is not good.
>
> Most people don't own a thing they have on all the way down to their shoes; they charged it. They're all flash and no cash.
>
> When you have done those calculations in prayerful and repentant determination, God will get you out of debt before your debt-free date.

My motto is:
If you can't pay something, say something.

Money should not be saved for emergencies.
Peek-a-boo!

Okay! Okay! I'll stop! I just love his down home way of teaching. Wouldn't you know it? He's originally a Texan too!

By the time your child asks for her first quarter to ride the carousel at the grocery store entrance, she is expressing her readiness for Financial Training 101. It is a child's tendency to admire beauty, and such a visit to the store usually creates a desire to acquire it. Most parents would want to satisfy her wish out of love for her. But what is the child thinking about the gifts her parents so lavishly heap on her? Is she just glad her desires are being met, or does she, as intended, really see these offerings as selfless acts of love? Here's how one family found resolution.

One of my clients wondered how to overcome their son's need for involvement in managing their holdings. As I talked with husband and wife, I soon realized that practically everything in their son's life was being done for him. The groundskeepers, housekeepers, and other staff maintained the estate leaving the child with little influence in his own environment. Yet, with all there was to do just to maintain their home, he still had a tremendous opportunity to experience the satisfaction of a job well done.

What might you have said to these concerned parents? Would you suggest that they reduce the staff to allow their son more opportunities to contribute to the family's lifestyle? Or would you have thought to have their child do a little labor, and scale back on some of the luxury inherent in living large? How might you offer to empower him?

Rather than suggesting to my client what their family should choose, I decided to look for opportunities along with them that were in keeping with the long-term parenting goals they had established. I learned a great deal from their answers to the initial intake. Their desire was for their son to have a positive outlook on life while learning to acquire, appreciate, and manage his own things and eventually, their estate.

I considered the input I had heard from the family. As it appeared that the home was being run around him, I asked, "Given your compelling desire to see your son assume greater responsibility, how could he participate as your protégé?" From this question, they developed the idea of co-coordinating the staff duties with their son. This included him actually planning for both their short and long-term estate needs along with distributing appropriate assignments to the staff. The parents were overjoyed with the concept of their son becoming their understudy. Consider *your* child's strength's and weaknesses and how to best optimize their potential.

While in some families, grooming this young man to learn from the ground up would have been appropriate, for this family it would have been disquieting. Thus, solutions and outcomes can vary to suit each particular family's needs. This clearly demonstrates the difference between a clinical vs. a life-coaching approach—the individuality of the solution reflects the needs and goals of the members involved.

In your family business plan (assuming you've developed one), if one of your parenting goals is to empower your children's success potential, you also would do well to think creatively. After all, what is homegrown leadership worth to you?

While we're on the subject, one of the first assignments my mentor gave me was to read the book *The Real Guide to Making Millions through Real Estate* by Lisa A. Vander. Had I had these kind of resources available to me earlier in life, my husband and I would not have purchased a primary residence and allowed the equity to be wasted for over a decade—especially since we live in one of the wealthiest property states in the nation! The second critical piece of input, along with making attending seminars a lifestyle, was to develop my core team and start using what I learned. So now that my skills are being honed, the future is looking much brighter for my family. We have already begun to give official authority to our children well in advance of our "home going." Now that's what I call empowerment!

Stop for a minute and consider the following:

- 141,606,000 women with children live in the United States
- 6.2 million businesses are women-owned
- Women-owned businesses generate $1.15 trilion in sales.
- Women-owned businesses employ 9.2 million people.

That's power! Yet it is my observation that the savviest of all of us will not encounter a more challenging or a more rewarding profession than family building. When it comes to making important decisions, your child may well be learning from you how to value others, themselves, and their money. What blueprint will you leave for your young apprentice to follow? Here's a thought that you may find of value as your child learns to master the art of wealth management.

First they gotta learn it!
Then they gotta earn it!
Then they gotta return it!
— Mark Victor Hansen

5

Learn To Think Past the School Setting

Day-dreaming is a crucial element of a well-rounded childhood and can be a way of us reconnecting with our own core values as adults. Over-crowded schedules, financial decisions, career challenges, and a number of other concerns often vie for our time. It isn't often that we allow ourselves to fantasize about creating the family life we've always wanted, much less taking the steps to make it a reality. So, can I challenge you to think about what a winning, fearless and fully functional family—yours—might look like?

Sometimes the smallest of adjustments can pull your family into alignment. One day some time back, a couple contacted me after discovering my website. Their child was exhibiting extreme behavior patterns, and they were deeply concerned. They were frustrated by the constraints of full-time work schedules that inhibited the time required for them to respond effectively. In our first session, Mom admitted that she wasn't coping well and that she often resorted to yelling. She was experiencing migraine headaches and was feeling a great deal of stress. This parent also told me that she was unable to relax, which scared her a little. Here is a portion of our dialogue during their initial coaching session. We started with her husband:

Me:	*What would you like to see in your child's character one year from now?*
Dad:	*I want my child to stop whining.*
Me:	*That's what you don't want to see. Now, what would you like to see a year from now?*
Dad:	*I'd like to see her stop bouncing off the walls so much.*
Me:	*Still, the focus is on the negative. Let me state this a little differently. What is the one thing you did not have growing up that you dream of giving to your little one?*
Dad:	*More stability!*
Me:	*Wow! That's huge! Mom, how about you?*
Mom:	*Well, I'd like to see her exhibit more self-control, the ability to focus, and be consistent.*

After allowing these parents to ponder over these thoughts for a week, here's how our next appointment went (bear in mind that a family's focus can shift from one session to the next):

Mom: *Mornings are always a problem.*

Me: *Then let's see how an opportunity can be created out of it. I'll do the hard part of generating a pros and cons list. You share your morning routine with me, and then we can break it down.*

Mom: *You mean every little thing we do?*

Me: *Yes. Please bear with me. I don't want to preempt your responses by telling you where I'm headed with this. So, Yes! Please tell me in detail.*

Mom: *Well, we wake up. I get ready for my day. I need more time to get ready, as I work in a formal setting. My husband spends more time with the children in the morning, because he can get ready in five minutes. He drops the girls off.*

Me: *Tell me about the routine for the children's dressing, hair....*

Dad: *I usually have to spend more time with that part of getting ready. My wife will help with one child while I work with the other. Then I usually just give them a glass or two of milk. They don't eat breakfast.*

Mom: *We have never eaten breakfast! Their daycare used to go all out with breakfast, so I never had to worry about it. Now that they're in preschool, they aren't given the big breakfast. So I've started making them a bag of dry cereal that they can at least take with them. I know I should do better than this! I know I have failed at this!*

Me: *I hope you understand that there is no judgment being made about you. There is no failure in this alliance, only opportunities to improve. There are no wrong responses here, and if my intonations are giving you that impression, let me correct that now. We are here to dream about where you want to see your family go from here.*

Mom: *I understand—I just know that I should be doing more. Actually, let me confess that I used to do it all by myself. But now that my husband is helping, I have been using the time to sleep in an extra 30 minutes in the morning.*

At this point, I reminded Mom of some of the long-term goals that she had identified in an assignment I had given during our initial session. I continued to ask more targeted questions. Soon, Mom discovered a small window of additional time that she could spend with the family in her morning schedule—even if it meant a bit less sleep. Once we created a safe space in which Mom and Dad could dream about winning as a family, they began to place a higher value on their family's wellbeing.

After just two weeks of coaching, the family began showing signs of a more peaceful home life. And as that continued, their child—the one for whom our alliance was initially created—was even feeling safe enough to address some of her concerns without ever being approached directly. It was a simple matter of the parents assessing their goals and reprioritizing their lives in ways that would allow them greater access to their own ideals.

This is another example of what can happen when fearless parents are willing to invest time and resources necessary to make the most of a mastermind group, or think tank. As they continued to develop consistency, I was pleased to learn that their family tapestry was beginning to take on a more beautiful appearance.

How Do You Envision Your Child in the Future?

What uncommon traits in your child's character do you most want him to hold on to? What do you see your offspring contributing some day? How can parents learn what is behind their preschooler's behavior? Wouldn't it be wonderful to find the answers without diminishing who the children were created to be?

Historically, schools have applied pressure to parents to respond to their children's uniqueness in ways that have gone against the grain. It turns out, however, that parents have not always seen their children's quirkiness as impairing, and some parents have even pulled their children out of schools that have. Einstein, Newton, and a host of others might have been given Individual Education Plans, or IEPs, and some of these greats might well have been medicated. Yet their families stubbornly hung on to their belief in their children's strengths. Now, whenever I turn on a switch in a room, I am reminded that a child with "very special needs" later came to invent that light-bulb concept. I often wonder where we'd be if such children were in our public schools today.

When I am initiating an alliance with a family, one of the first things I look for is something in the child's surroundings that could be creating an imbalance. It may seem unbelievable, but I have yet to find a child who is "the problem." There are often external factors that are upsetting their keen sense of well-being. I also look to the child's unique abilities and interests to see how they dovetail, or don't, when compared with their home or other current learning environment and the setting in which the child functions.

A Dream Worth Revisiting

Have we changed that much, or could something else be contributing to the downward shift in our family values? I recently polled no fewer than 100 people on this question, and found that the responses were age-related and culturally dependent. Many from the older generation (including some who were foreign-born) shared that creating a secure home environment was their number one priority. Baby boomers, on the other hand, seemed more in favor of diving into their careers and juggling the rest of life.

What has changed our attitude toward the family? I asked a very successful working mother to share what she thought about this remarkable phenomenon. These were her thoughts:

"In the late 50s and early 60s, we were very optimistic. It seemed as if everyone was getting the newest appliances: a garbage disposal, dishwasher, or freezer. The American Dream was a reality. Houses were cheap, and if you had a job you were likely able to buy one. Science and technology were rapidly replacing traditional values, and this was viewed as progress.

"Everyone, or almost everyone, was an evolutionist. Christians wove all kinds of compromises into their views of origin. We were led to believe that technology would free women from housework. And it has. Before my grandmothers even started washing clothes in a tub with a washboard, women had to first draw the water usually with a hand pump and then heat it on a wood-burning stove. Before Proctor and Gamble, women also had to make their own soap. Prior to the 50s, many households did not have running water. My grandparents didn't until around 1956.

"Then after being recruited into the workforce during World War II, women began to pursue careers, and it was at that point that they started trying to balance children, a husband, a home, and a career. The workweek was supposed to be 20-30 hours by that time. The daycare centers for children that were springing up everywhere were viewed as positive places for learning and social interaction. "

In this example it was advances in technology that seemed to lead to the shift away from the American family being the center of society. Could additional factors also have been catalysts? Consider another side of the elephant as described by an equally accomplished woman business owner.

During World War II women, of necessity, joined the workforce en masse. It was for the greater good that they replaced the men who had been called to war. For many of them, returning to hearth and home was difficult. They had become breadwinners, and with the return of their men, they were once again supposed to become the nurturers.

More and more women began going to college, and they began infiltrating careers formerly the province of men. The numbers of female doctors and lawyers grew exponentially as did the numbers of women in other formerly male-dominated jobs. The ERA became a political football.

Along with this change came the Pill and the Sexual Revolution. Again, women were faced with what appeared to be new freedoms. And as with any new freedoms, there was overindulgence...

With the late 1960's the days of counting only the husband's salary on a mortgage application became a thing of the past. Where it was previously thought that once a wife became pregnant, she would stay at home to raise her child, the late 1960's saw a new attitude. Women were in the workplace to stay. And with this, and the application of their income to the mortgage decision-making process, the cost of houses escalated.

Simultaneously, Madison Avenue was telling women they could, "...bring home the bacon, fry it up in a pan, and never let him forget he's a man..." while over-looking what this would mean to the children and the family structure as a whole.

Women had sought and gained the freedom to join the workforce; now society had found a way to shackle many of them to it. We often forget that there is a cost to everything, and for many women career freedom has now camouflaged itself as being necessary!

My mother-in-law's life-long career was in raising her 12 children. In our day, she would be considered an anomaly. After all, assuming that you have ideal sur-roundings and the best possible support-system, would you sacrifice your own ambitions to care for your chil-dren? These days, it's highly unlikely!

If you work away from home, and you have chil-dren, you probably utilize another caregiver. Most still choose their own family members first, but in this age of insulated families, that child care is sometimes left to strangers. What are some of the most important con-cerns you might have in delegating the care-giving role for your children to someone else?

- A belief system similar to your own?
- An optimal approach to health and nutrition?
- A caregiver who has children of his/her own?
- A provider whose personal lifestyle choices complement yours?
- An environment that will nurture your child emotionally, intellectually, and spiritually?
- A safe and secure environment? How will you know?

In listening to parents with young children, I find that some recognize the significance of these kinds of questions only after their choice in childcare has gone sour. But there is hope.

The Internet revolution has created an opportunity for women to work from home while attending to the needs of their families. Businesses are seeing the advantages in being able to retain higher quality staff, and in the increased productivity of that staff. Home-based ventures run by women and Mompreneurs are no longer frowned upon, but comprise the fastest growing market segment according to the May, 2007 issue of the *Costco Connection*. In fact a whole new cottage industry has developed to support their unique requirements. Even the book you are now holding in your hands provides an example of the kind of resources being generated by Mompreneurs, including yours truly. Thanks for your support!

No Child Grips Our Heart Like Our Own!

Some stereotypes die hard. And, unfortunately for all of us, the one about stay-at-home mothers has a powerful influence on the choices many women make.

"I'm not just some homemaker sitting around the house in my bathrobe all day watching soap operas," said my professor defensively during a lecture in child development. "I'm a college professor and a single parent raising my adopted daughter!" Her doctoral degree was in child development.

Where have I been? I thought to myself, nearly choking on what I was hearing. I seemed to have missed something in the years I had been away from college. Now, as a student returning to the academic culture, I was shocked at this professor's words. Isn't the invested parent's home the place where healthy children first begin to thrive?

Ever since junior high school, I held a reputation for being the one willing to ask the tough questions. I had repeatedly taken the heat for speaking up, yet I could not dismiss the notion that we were in class to learn. Since no one else voiced disagreement with the instructor, I could not let this important learning opportunity pass without asking the professor for clarification. I felt the sting of assault in my chosen role as a homebuilder, and quickly overcame my fear and said, "I'm confused by your statement. I'm one of those homemakers you spoke about. Personally, we don't even own a television set. I am in your class because, as a homemaker, I am privileged to spend my time as I am inclined to."

My professor's tone suddenly changed as she began to tell of the hardships of being a single parent. What she really wished, she reflected, was that she had the support of a husband like mine. What the professor was doing was thinking aloud about her choice to adopt a baby by herself. After discovering first hand the painful inequity in opting for a husband-free family, she was expressing some bitter feelings. What surprised me most was that a professor whose focus was child development had not reflected on this life-changing option ahead of time.

In the beginning, my line of work often required me to observe programs all across the county. It is my professional finding that all too many of our children and their "qualified" staff are desperately struggling with full-time care. It appears to be a universal truth that when mothers choose to turn their children over to others, whether child expert or not, they are likely to experience gut-wrenching emotions as a result.

"Who takes the child by the hand,
takes the mother by the heart."
Danish Proverb

One Size May Not Fit All

Listening to our children and actually hearing what they are trying to say are often two different things. As parents, we need to hear our children in their language and from their own unique perspective, and to realize that perspective may impact what they glean from what we say.

Some children thrive in a care-giving environment. It is pretty certain that all children will thrive in the environment that is right for them. One that is just the right size. Puppy size perhaps?

"Puppy size! She keeps repeating it over and over again," the woman told the volunteer. "We have been to this shelter at least five times in the last few weeks."

"What is it that she is asking for?" the volunteer asked.

"Puppy size!"

"Well, we have plenty of puppies, and they are all different sizes, if that's what she's looking for."

"I know. We've seen most of them," the Mom said in frustration.

Just then, the young child came walking into the office.

"Well, did you find one?" the mother asked.

"No, not this time," the child said sadly. "Can we come back on the weekend?" The two women looked at each other, shook their heads and laughed.

"We never know when we will get more dogs," said the volunteer. "Unfortunately, there's always a supply."

The young child took her mother by the hand and headed toward the door. "Don't worry, I bet we'll find one this weekend," she said.

Over the next few days, both Mom and Dad had long conversations with her. They both felt she was being too particular.

"It will be this weekend," said her father in frustration, "because we're not looking any more."

"We don't want to hear another word about 'puppy size' either," added Mom.

When the weekend came, the Mom and daughter returned to the shelter. By now, the young child knew her way around, so she ran right to the section that housed the puppies. Tired of the routine, Mom sat in the small waiting room at the end of the first row of cages. One by one the dogs were brought out to the girl. And one by one, she said, "Sorry, you're not the one."

It was the last cage on this last day in search of the perfect pup. The volunteer opened the cage door, and the child carefully picked up the dog and held it close. This time she took a little longer.

"Mom, this is him! I found the right puppy! He's the one! I know it!" She screamed with joy.

Mom, startled by all the commotion, came running. "What? Are you sure? How do you know?" she asked.

"It's the puppy sighs!"

"But it's the same size as all the other puppies you held the last few weeks," Mom said.

"No, not size—sighs," the child said. "When I held him in my arms, he sighed. Don't you remember? When I asked you one day what love is, you told me that love depends on the sighs of your heart. The more you love, the bigger the sighs!"

The two women looked at each other for a moment. Mom didn't know whether to laugh or cry. As she stooped down to hug her child, she did a little of both.

"Mom, every time you hold me, I sigh. When you and Daddy come home from work and hug each other, you both sigh. I knew I would find the right puppy if it sighed when I held it in my arms," she said. Then, holding the puppy up close to her face, she said, "Mom, he loves me. I heard the sighs of his heart."

We may listen often to our children, but it is important that we take the time to really hear what they have to say. In hearing, we learn who they are and, just as importantly, how we affect who they will become.

6

Motivation is More Caught Than Taught

Ever feel like you're just not seeing things clearly? Almost like you're squinting in a fog or peering through a mist, knowing that it won't be long before the weather clears and the sun shines again?

Sometimes We Need an Aerial View to See Past the Trees

When parents first approach a coaching session, they are often uncertain as to what to expect. Sometimes, the answers they seek have been waiting to be discovered for some time. One television personality has made a career out of helping parents see their children in a new way through the use of consistent discipline, rewards, and involvement in their children's lives. She is known as the "Super Nanny," and her television show has a wide following.

When clients first come to me, they are often surprised to discover that their intake packet is anything but behavior-specific. It includes all kinds of seemingly off the wall questions about their views on the overall wellbeing of the child and the family, and very little about the child's problems or school setting. I have done this intentionally, because I believe that restoring the child's balance is contingent on their entire "wheel of life." In getting to the bottom line, I find it limiting to isolate the child from any aspect of his or her environment. That's because all aspects of a child's environment impact their behavior, and my coaching centers around creating a safe environment in which the child and the family can thrive.

It generally takes three to six months of consecutive weekly sessions for clients to reach one or more of their target goals. In the beginning, we review in depth the entire family environment and what they dream it will be when we're finished; it is at this juncture that they set their goals. My intent is to help them envision their ideal family, and then map out a plan for how they will get there—and then to coach them to their desired goal line. Here are some of the questions that often get flushed out in the beginning:

- What will the result of our coaching alliance yield for the child & family?
- How committed are the parents to working to achieve their end result?
- In the alliance, how do they see my posture best supporting their success?

I also use an in depth questionnaire that is designed to stir the parent's thinking about their family life. It is designed to help parents see that more often than they think, unexplained behaviors (frizzamyers) in children can be motivated by the family's beliefs, interactions, dynamics, and values. I have found that children's behaviors and parental interests often overlap in peculiar ways. The areas from the "wheel of life" that are covered can include:

- The learning environment
- Money matters
- Parental relationships
- Peer associations
- Physical health status
- Purpose of their life
- Sibling interactions
- Spiritual development

I then support the parents as they record measurable short-term and long-term goals for their child(ren) and for themselves. *The Fearless Parenting Audio* Series covers a number of these same areas in much greater depth, with a primary emphasis on physical health status. Please check it out at *www.fearlessparenting.com*. But let me warn you. I don't want you to be taken off guard by the emotion this series is intended to invoke in you. Try it risk-free for just two weeks. You'll come out on the other end a fearless parent, or I'll give back every dime you've paid!

Not My Mother, Not My Sister, But It's Me, Oh Lord!

Even as adults, we are prey to insecurities and frizzamyers, the effect of which trickle down. The complexity of our human nature can impact even the youngest family members. The following scenario comes from my private journal. I see most mothers relating to it while some dad's may find it eye-opening. Even a few may find it helpful in better understanding their wives. By being transparent, I am trying to demonstrate how my state of being influences not only me but also my husband and even my youngest child as well. This is why I prefer to coach in the family context regardless of the reason my services are retained.

> Seeing me upset makes my baby daughter, Dree, cry. When she observes me even beginning to get upset, she quickly flashes a smile to try and alter my mood. Who is this child who only met me face-to-face a few weeks ago, yet already knows me so well, who is so attuned to the fluctuations in my moods?

Like many mothers, I was particularly emotional after her birth. While she couldn't possibly understand how I felt after my husband started back to work after being with us for several weeks after her birth, she was privy nonetheless to my emotional upheaval once we were left on our own. She didn't know that I had felt less attractive since her birth. She didn't care that I didn't feel sexy anymore. She was blissfully unaware that while part of me was missing her dad, part of me was also simultaneously fearful of him finding people at work more interesting and being envious of his freedom to be "out" in the workplace. But she was still affected by all of my mixed emotions.

After thinking back on those days, I realize that even though friends told me that I should sleep when she did, instead, I typically scrambled to get things done. I washed the dishes, did the laundry, replied to e-mails, answered my voicemails, prepared meals, and so on. No wonder I didn't feel sexy! My personal appearance was an afterthought. I didn't have time for me. Exhausted, Peter and I usually ended up falling asleep each night just holding on to each other. My frizzamyers got the best of me, and little Dree sensed it.

The days when I engaged my support system, the tough places felt so much smoother. Three mornings each week, at 5:00 a.m., my girlfriends scooped Dree and me up for an early morning hike. They reminded me that everything going on in my confused and hectic life was quite normal. I realized then that in the future, when I got stuck, the best thing to do would be dial a date with a friend instead of isolating myself and letting Dree feel the strain of my frustrations. To this day, this works for me. What works best for you?

Even when we know better, as parents we can fall prey to the frustrations inherent in being accountable to and for our children. Babies unknowingly offer a vivid reminder of our own need to feel nurtured as parents. It's kind of like the instructions the flight attendants give to put on our facemask in an emergency before assisting someone else. We can't help another person when our own sense of wellbeing is at risk of being, or is already compromised. So, while reaching out in your time of need can seem invasive and thoroughly uncomfortable, having the support of friends and family—and sometimes a coach—is vital to new parents (fathers included) and remains important as our children grow.

The process of adjusting to our new baby took months, but little by little stresses were replaced by peace. Day after day, our baby girl was being blessed by the improvements. Now, Dree doesn't need to encourage me to smile anymore, because I smile a lot. She and I are both thriving.

Unexpressed emotions can be like quicksand, and as parents we can be dragged down into them before we realize what is happening. Our children's frizzamyers at times result from our own internal state as well as our personal/peer interactions. Engaging the input of compassionate people, even if only to reassure us that what we are feeling is not unique, can make all the difference in the world. Yes, this coach has needed coaching too! In fact, most of the better coaches will likely have one.

How might your life be affecting your child? What do you observe about the health of the relationships you have established? How have they influenced your involvement at home? Does inspiration spill over into your family? What do you observe about your children's behavior? Can it be linked to conditions that are present in your life?

Our difficulties, challenges, and even many of our stressors are often indicators letting us know that it is time to let go even more so we can grow again. Hopefully, you will be able to respond with creativity to the opportunities that life presents. You, too, may find it beneficial to brainstorm possible solutions with your friends or the life coach who holds you accountable. Failing forward has become one of my favorite mottos.

The Village People

Peter and I have carefully chosen those who will help us guide our family toward its full potential. Our support system is unmatched and has been tested more than once, most recently, as I have discussed, by the arrival of our little baby, Dree. Peter and I were married many years before she came along. By then our son was fully grown. Her arrival, while joyful, meant a lot would change.

My best friend, seeing that Peter and I were thoroughly exhausted, stayed over one night to take the baby off our hands. She has not failed to drop in anytime she has sensed a need in our home. Another very close friend routinely gives me feedback regarding the care and decorating of our home, including accessories, paint colors, landscape design, and more. A good friend of my husband's came alongside to help us with remodeling projects around the house—or should I say we helped him? Massage therapy and housekeeping provided by our adopted grandparents have been a Godsend.

I could go on and on talking about the blessings of my true friends.

It's been said that it takes a village to raise a child. What it really takes is strong, loving parents. And often our ability to parent with patience and consistency is augmented by the support of loving, caring friends and family in tune with our values. In that sense, together we can make um thrive!

> *"A true friend is the greatest of all blessings, and that which we take the least care of all to acquire."*
> La Rochefoucauld, Maxims (1665)

Do You See What I See?

Now it's time for you to sit back and consider your influence on your spouse, child(ren), and other loved ones. Think about which of those relationships is the most prominent in your life right now. Who is pressing on your heart as you read this book? Identify at least 3 key areas of importance in this relationship. Some areas will hopefully be positive, while others may present opportunities for improvement. Use the "Pros" column that follows to record the strengths that bind you together. Then write down those areas that need attention in the "Pre-Pros" column on the following page. As you recall what works well and how you can bring other interactions up to a healthier level, you may gain a sense of relief in taking actual steps toward making your lives together even better!

PROS	PRE-PROS

7

Get Engaged in What Truly Inspires!

How we influence our children's lives is as much—or more—from what we do as it is from what we say. Our actions, and our inactions, can impact their health and well-being; can impact their intellectual growth; can be a major force in determining whether or not they fulfill their unique potential. And that influence is asserted both directly and indirectly! How are you influencing and inspiring your children? How are you inspiring in them a healthy lifestyle?

These days, it seems as if every one is talking about the obesity epidemic. Some of the wisdom behind prevention reaches far beyond physical weight. What is the earliest we can influence our child's likelihood of becoming obese? Could it even be as soon as, if not prior to birth? Just to be a little different, and to stay in touch with my own special needs, I thought we'd talk about how to motivate our family to adapt a lifestyle that is healthier overall. More learning is caught than taught, and one way to encourage optimal choices in children is to model them for our own well being.

The parent's choice about whether to breastfeed their baby is one place to start. Many new mothers learn quickly that they must be highly motivated to stick with breastfeeding, especially in the beginning. Parents do well to understand that breast tenderness, having enough milk, and more can be easily overcome through well matched educational support. The option of seeing our baby's second and third birthday in good health can make the choice to breastfeed worth the effort. Nursing helps to develop a healthy immune system in a child. The American Academy of Pediatrics and the World Health Organization agree that including breast milk in our child's diet through and even beyond the first year is wise. There is even some evidence that breastfeeding helps a new mother avoid postpartum depression. There is one more great reason for breastfeeding. Breastfed babies are less likely to be obese. I'm certainly watching this one unfold since Dree l-o-v-e-s to eat! ☺

From the beginning, parents are foundational in their children's development, and this theme seems to continue throughout the child-rearing years. This is clearly evident in many areas of life, including schools where physical fitness is no longer valued for its ability to increase positive endorphins, improve attentiveness, and contribute to healthier interactions overall. And especially preschools where during one of the child's most active stages of development, physical activity is reduced to an extra curricular activity or a break from the monotony of classroom time. If ever there was a time to motivate our children toward developing health-filled habits, including a passion for being physically active, that time would ideally be when they are first starting to internalize their approach to life outside the womb.

Health Facts to Motivate You

How does motivation contribute to our ability to be our children's example? Well, if you've ever known someone who has struggled with moving past the poor health choices he or she has made in the past, you may have noticed that person trying every fad imaginable only to return to the same stale place of defeat. Having a good plan can help us get started on living well. But knowledge alone may not be enough to keep us on track. We sometimes need ongoing emotional support so we can maintain our successes. Now let's talk about some basics for good health.

Water to Stay Imbalanced?

Give your child good hydration habits! Water is crucial to our wellbeing. Good, clean, additive-free water is essential to our health and the health of our children. It has been said that we have the ability to live for weeks without food, but only three days without water. Our bodies use it differently depending on a host of factors, including our stage of life. Surprisingly the water content in our body is at its best when it is way out of balance, kind of like the land to water ratio of the earth. For example it is believed that:

- infants are made of approximately 80 percent water
- teens around 70 percent, and
- the elderly around 50 percent

If you or your child have a headache, do you immediately reach for an analgesic, or do you first think about how much water you have or haven't had? Do you notice how much younger your skin looks when you keep hydrated? Or how much better your digestive system works?

Look at the shopping carts around you in the grocery store, and look in your own refrigerator. If carbonated beverages abound, something is amiss. Our children need calcium to grow on. Carbonated beverages leach that calcium from their systems. Studies also show that children who drink carbonated beverages, even sugar-free ones, are more disposed to indulge in sugar and to be overweight. You don't want to miss what David Kennedy, DDS, adds to the section on physical health status in the *Fearless Parenting Audio* Series.

If you have chosen not to nurse your children, are you choosing your alternatives carefully? Formula can impact more than our children's weight; reaction to soy formula can disrupt the delicate hormonal balance in our babies. This knowledge is not new. It goes back to studies done by George Washington Carver. Hormones are also present in the meat we eat and the dairy products we consume because our livestock is fed hormones. Consumption of these hormones can dramatically impact the development of our children. Studies show how highly concentrated hormones in food are reportedly producing all the signs of puberty in today's preschool-aged children. Board Certified Clinical Nutritionist David Getoff responds to this issue in the physical health status section of the Fearless Parenting Audio Series. Shhh! Don't tell your dietician I told you about it.

Then there are the chemicals, some of which are banned in other countries, that remain central ingredients in our consumption rituals. Do you purchase organicially grown foods for your family? Is your kitchen a hormone, pesticide, additive-free zone? No child needs these neurotoxins or hormonal disruptors in their bodies.

Does your family experience the rewards of staying hydrated and chemical free?

Food That Gives Life

Americans reportedly spend an average of one trillion dollars per year on managing diseases. In 2000 alone, research showed that our society spent three billion dollars on prescription drugs, while 90 percent of our food budget went for the purchase of processed substances and chemical replacements for nutrients. Doesn't it stand to reason that along with the consumption of life-subtracting substances, we can expect dis-ease to eventually follow?

So how is it that a child can be given only organic foods, be taking the "right" supplements, yet still not feel physically well? Perhaps there is more involved than just food consumption.

Compare your morning routine to how your body has been designed to experience it. It is in the morning, between 7 A.M. and 9 A.M. that our stomachs hit their peak in energy function. This suggests that breakfast (which literally means "breaking the fast") is vitally important in sustaining us well. Help your family, both adults and children, break the fast with a nutritious breakfast. This should not be determined based on its ability to fit conveniently into your lifestyle but as an adhesive in maintaining your family's health. This is not a luxury; it is a necessity of health.

Sensing Your Way Toward Optimal Health

Our senses, and those of our children, respond either positively or negatively to stimuli, and that stimuli informs our mood.

What sounds awaken your home and family in the morning? The first utterances your family wakes up to are important. I've been taught that water takes on the form of what contains it. But it has been proven that tones can also shape molecules in water. Consider this quote from *The Secret Life of Plants* by Dr. Lee Lorenzen: "Plant physiology reacts dramatically to the sound of the human voice. Words, both positive and negative, produce profound changes in water flow dynamics." Being made of mostly water, no wonder it so happens that when my family compliments me, I almost melt with pleasure.

So, does your home come alive to the sound of praise and worship and other melodic tones to uplift your family's spirits? If not, consider creating new rituals that can restore harmony inside your home. You might soon be overjoyed with the outcome. You and your family will certainly get off to a better start each day!

What sights awaken you each morning? The way that you greet each other first thing can set the tone for the rest of your day. Does the TV, a video, or some other less disarming vision welcome your family into their new day? Or is it the warm smile of a trusted relative?

What smells stimulate your loved ones in the morning? Did you know that before you even take your first bite, the aroma of nourishing food being prepared engages the salivary glands and prepares your digestive enzymes to process your breakfast more efficiently?

What tastes start your family on the road to optimum health? Parents can cultivate a well rounded pallet in their children by focusing on colors, textures, shapes, and the 5 more basic flavors: sweet, sour, bitter, spicy, and salty. Since taste is learned, children who are exposed to new foods on a weekly basis are less likely to be picky eaters, or to develop food sensitivity. Because Dree has a delicate digestive system, our acupuncturist recommended greatly limiting variability in her meals for 2 to 3 years until her digestive system has matured. So consult your provider about your family's specific needs.

There is a worthwhile family movement that erupted after the fast food industry started spreading its tentacles oversees. Visit: *www.slowfoodusa.org*.

Flavors, Textures, Colors...Oh My!

For most of us, the notion of wellbeing is a murky one where the family's welfare may be compromised by drugs, genetically modified food, and a myriad of chemical substitutes for whole food. The labels on processed foods offer an example of how many chemicals we are taking in. Providers I know who practice outside of the framework of dis-ease management tell me that they are finding chronic ailments much less responsive to treatment due to the composition of the toxins that now block our normal healing process.

When it comes to the food choices for my family, wherever possible I avoid processed foods in favor of fresh, organic, free range, vine ripened... and I include a wide array of textures, colors, and flavors. I also add a lot of dried and fresh cut raw herbs to complement and bring zest to most meals.

> *"See I have given you every herb that yields seed*
> *which is on the face of all the earth,*
> *and every tree whose fruit yields seed;*
> *to you it shall be for food"*
> The Master Chef (Genesis 1:29, OEM).

The objective our Creator had in mind seems to have been our consumption of live foods that either produced or contained seeds. My nutritional mentor told me of a countywide science fair he judged in which a high school student produced an analyzer that registered the vitamin content of fresh fruit. He plucked an orange from a tree and found it to contain some 10,000 milligrams of vitamin C. One hour later, retesting the same piece of water-soluble fruit revealed that it had lost nearly all but 10 milligrams of its original vitamin C potency (Note that most of the vitamin C in oranges has been shown to be in the white layer just beneath the outer skin). We personally experienced this when Dree was catching a cold. Oranges were in season, and without the foreknowledge of their value she just kept picking the ones low enough on the tree for her to reach and eating them one after another. I found this quite fascinating to watch because within an hour her symptoms were gone.

Viewing this concept from yet another angle, as mentioned earlier I understand there to be at least five main tastes that our palates are beautifully suited to enjoy. I can readily identify 3 of these flavors in just one food group—herbs:

HERBS	
Sweet	Stevia
Bitter	Dark leaf lettuce varieties
Spicy	Arugula

So here in just one food group you have three of the five tastes: sweet, bitter, and spicy. Can you think of others?

Caring for the Littlest Ones

While directing a child development center for some 200 children, I noticed that all but one of them experienced sickness. So when the one child who had avoided getting sick developed symptoms, I attempted to determine the cause. First I learned that while the staff had been trained to wash the young children's hands as a preventative measure to stop the spread of germs, they were not washing the babies' hands. We cleaned and sterilized everything we could at the end of each day. But while we had the drill down to a science, the thought had never occurred to me to get the staff and the parents to also include our infants. Then when the one child who seemed somehow immune caught her first cold, I approached the parent out of curiosity. The mom of this infant confided that the peer pressure of being the only one breastfeeding had become too much for her, and, as a result, she had allowed her milk to dry up and began formula feeding instead. Although easily intimidated, the parent was quite savvy in pointing me directly to the root of why her baby had a cold. Wow! What an incredible miracle! The immuno-globulin factors in her milk were actually protecting her baby's immune system from all the disease carrying elements she was exposed to in our center. Having to learn from an infant what strengthened her undeveloped immune system left me quite humbled.

While it is each parent's right to choose how to best feed and nurture their child, the research provides compelling arguments in favor of nursing for at least the first nine months—particularly if that child will be in day care.

First, Do No Harm!

We are conditioned to trust professionals, including medical practitioners: doctors, nurses, pharmacists, psychiatrists, psychologists, physical therapists, etc.

One of the most surprising findings from my days of working in childhood mental illness is just who determines which drugs get issued to the young. My assumption had always been that a physician's responsibility required him or her to accurately determine which meds were designed for whom and to dispense medications with great care. But that couldn't have been further from the truth. Most doctors prescribe drugs for children based on information they receive from drug-company trained pharmaceutical representatives. How can this be?

After a visit from a concerned patient, one physician whom I served began a research quest that caught my attention. Discovering that a certain drug was associated with a particular eye disease, this doctor became concerned and asked a pharmaceutical rep about the matter. The following scene unfolded like an Alfred Hitchcock movie.

As the physician recounted the event, the rep's expression went from sugary sweet to that of a rigid disciplinarian. He said, "You were not authorized to do that!" referring to the doctor's research efforts. "WHO TOLD YOU TO DO THAT?" The doctor looked at me in disbelief, and I am sure I returned an astonished expression. Gathering inner strength, the provider responded, "I did it on my own!" Then there was silence.

I don't remember whether the two went behind closed doors to resolve their differences or if they just dropped the subject. I was already mentally thinking of questions.

What kind of industry was this? How were pharmaceutical reps any different from the drug dealers I had grown up around? On second thought, maybe they were even worse than street dealers. I remember seeing intimidating faxes coming into a pharmacy in which I was consulting, warning the proprietor about getting his quota of drug sales up by the end of the month...or else! Then there were those telling documents that came through the doctor's offices every now and then, like the one about Vioxx that many seemed to ignore. Just before it was yanked off the market, Vioxx earned approval for use in children: *http://www.mercola.com/2004/oct/27/vioxx_kids.htm.* For a non-stop read on this topic check out *Confessions of a Former Drug Dealer* by Gwen Olsen, a book written by a former pharmaceutical company rep, which provides a first-hand account of the machinations of the pharmaceutical industry.

This reminded me of another phenomenon I had often witnessed. Drug reps would suggest that an adult drug be given to children for the purposes of experimentation. They offered incredible incentives to the physician willing to do so. But when a doctor tried to tell the rep about the outcomes of the drugs, the rep responded, "I AM NOT SUPPOSED TO BE HEARING THIS!"

> *Pharmacy: "1. ...drug, medicine, poison, magic potion,... to practice divination or magic..."*
> —Webster's *Third International Dictionary of the English Language* (1961)

Will the Real Parent Please Stand Up?

Just who is most qualified to decide the course of action for your son or daughter's healthcare? One recent survey asked doctors their thoughts? Of the nearly 900 polled nationwide, most believed that adults could make their own medical choices, but where children were concerned, 84 percent of doctors felt that they should have authority over parents.

"Monkey Nucleosis"

The next story is representative of many of the medicated preschool-age children I've coached. One of my five-year-old clients was posing a significant challenge for others. He suffered from sleep deprivation and a host of other prescription drug-related ailments. The parent explained that the boy was on high doses of Depakote™ and Seroquil™ and had also been prescribed Prozac™. This occurred after a frizzamyer (or "melt down") in the psychiatrist's office, when the child refused to get on the scale. Here is a portion of my interpretation of what happened based on the parent's explanation of the event.

"He refused to get on the scale and started screaming and kicking. He even kicked the doctor. We had to drag him to the scale!" said the mother.

When I learned that my client may have been fearful of returning to this medical setting, and given his reservations about getting on the scale, I wondered whether his fears had been addressed. It might have been that when his family chose to drag him to the scale, his behavior escalated. Could there have been a deficit in age-appropriate communication rather than the need for the titration (in this case adding) of more drugs? We know that Prozac is not regulated for use in patients under 18-years of age. Could the introduction of this medication (noted in adults for its disruption of sexual function, sleep, the intestines, nutrients...) also be contraindicated in our five-year old client?"

Here is a transcript portion of another of my sessions with him.

> Most of his education seems to be coming from an after-school cartoon that centers on someone having what was called "Monkey-Nucleosis." In the cartoon, the narrator stated that, 'Early physicians believed that even a

> touch could cause sweating, fever, irritability, loss of appetite, and the X.'
>
> After viewing the cartoon, the client told his parent (who had not been present in the T.V. room) that he had seen monsters and was afraid. The parent dismissed his fears by saying, "There are no monsters in my house. I don't see any monsters here. I keep my house safe."

What do you think this child might have been feeling? Do you think his will or spirit might have been impacted by his parent's dismissal of his fears and that those fears may have been carried by him into the doctor's office? What happened in the session above? Given the ongoing media and medical influences in this client's life, might his behavior at the doctor's office have made sense? Also to be considered is whether the fear induced by the child's media exposure, if handled differently by the parent, would have manifested differently. Or what would have happened if the parent more closely monitored what the child was exposed to on TV. How influential is the media in developing your child's character? Where are the television, Internet and video games placed in your home? Are these family activities that you engage in together or in isolation from one another?

Children need to know that their parents take them seriously. That they take their fears seriously. In doing so, a parent provides spiritual safety and reassurance. The fear of the doctor's office, in this case, was induced by the child's media exposure. The response of the parent to the child's initial outreach left the child feeling unsafe to communicate his fear of the doctor's office. Thus the frizzamyer.

This child's spirit was wounded. His spiritual health had been compromised by a combination of the media's destructive after-school cartoons, his parent's emotionally detached state, and psychiatric reinforcement that he was "the problem."

According to Piaget, our client might not have been able to comprehend what he saw on TV. He might have had difficulty properly comparing and contrasting it with his feelings. It seems that this cartoon was directed at an audience other than that of a pre-operational child, because at this stage the child may literally believe what he sees. He does not have the cognitive skills to analyze a cartoon and understand that it is fantasy. In fact, there was so much negative material in the animation that it might have been difficult even for a trained professional to protect a little one's concrete reasoning from the assault.

After a year of continually experimenting with medications and utilizing special education experts and therapists, our client's behavior remained unaltered. It was not surprising that he was in a special education class. My services were retained to address the violence this young child expressed toward his parent and others. After supporting him through coaching for a short while, a treatment team meeting was scheduled. The clinician repeatedly asked me, "How were you able to calm him? What have you been doing with him?" I explained that I had responded by only speaking to him with respect, and that we had set a few boundaries together in previous sessions.

Apparently these boundaries were precedents for this client. In our first session, he approached me as though he might become physical. I did not react. I considered that he was acting merely out of an investigative need to compare my response to that of his parent and the professionals in his world.

I always spoke softly so that he did not feel at fault, but I was also firm in explaining what I needed him to do and how I would respond in turn. We rehearsed scenes before they happened, providing him with the opportunity to consider his next move. Although he could muster up a sinister snarl, I fearlessly looked this dear frightened angel in the eyes with gentle reassurance. He quickly learned that I would remain consistent. Additionally, he honed his self-reliance skills during our sessions. This enabled him to maneuver in his environment regardless of where his parent was emotionally. Having prayed for him beforehand, I was in awe of how the Lord directed our sessions despite the parent's own personal inner turmoil. Needless to say, his well-being was soon restored.

This parent was in the middle of a divorce. She was depressed and taking medication, and her son experienced a detachment from her concurrent with her emotional state. As a parent on these meds, the mother seemed naturally predisposed to suggestions that medication would help her child. What this child really needed was an available, responsive, consistent adult who would hear what he had to say, and then lovingly guide him in safely assimilating it so that his spirit could find rest. In fulfilling that role, I helped restore his balance and medication for him proved unnecessary—although our outcomes failed to convince his psychiatrist of this.

After attending an educational conference on the extent of the current preschool crisis, one psychiatrist told me he was convinced that all of these children with behavioral problems should be medicated. It seems that many of our public school teachers and their administrators are of a similar mindset. From their initial evaluation, we find that most children with frizzamyers would be identified, permanently labeled, and medically treated. In all the observations I've done, I hardly recall a single child feeling that he had an option in such matters. Human experiments are supposed to require the subject's approval. But the children on whom we are experimentally using drugs meant for adults have no say—so in their treatment. And when the drugs are mandated by social services by way of the educational system, neither do the parents. This reliance on drugs to handle manifestations of environmental irritations in children has to stop. As fearless parents we need to band together to protect our children from these inhumane assaults on their health.

Pharm-Assist

Whatever a pregnant mother consumes is also ingested by the child she is carrying.

It had been a typical day in the pharmacy where I had been retained to consult on complementary health care. Business was humming along when a disturbing call came in. I was summoned to the pharmacist's desk. Being a nutritionist, I had no prior experience whatsoever in prescribing drugs.

The pharmacist looked frazzled and my heart went out to him even before I understood why I had been called over. He gave no details, but asked if I knew anything about a particular drug as it related to fetal development. It didn't take long for me to realize that a physician had prescribed a drug to a compliant pregnant patient, and now there were concerns over the family's safety. Both medical collaborators were scared. I think I was consulted due to my background as a pediatric health educator with the hospital. Or perhaps it was my savvy as a researcher. Whatever the reason, I immediately made a few phone calls. It was now after hours around the country, but I was blessed to be able to reach a live person at the Mayo Clinic who provided support to this worried pharmacist. It is my professional understanding that anything a mother consumes also nourishes her baby. I am continually amazed at the number of medical professionals who think otherwise. So, while we address medicating preschoolers and young children, we might consider also addressing how trusting pregnant women are being persuaded to begin medicating their young even prior to birth.

Orientation and Training

During my first visit to see my doctor for prenatal care, he told me that his only purpose in seeing me throughout my pregnancy was to watch for anything that might go wrong. And this is healthcare? I asked myself. Further evidence of a flawed medical system came when my girlfriend, a physical therapist, told me that she was being trained to perform post-operative procedures on patients. She said other hospitals had already begun to do the same because of the shortage of nurses.

First do no harm is an essential part of the Hippocratic Oath. But with medicine having become big business, and specialization removing more and more doctors from a holistic approach to health care, even with the best of intentions, medical practitioners are on a slippery slope. Here's what some medical researchers are saying..

"It is evident that the American medical system is the leading cause of death and injury in the United States...Medical science amasses tens of thousands of papers annually—each one a tiny fragment of the whole picture. To look at only one piece and try to understand the benefits and risks is to stand one inch away from an elephant and describe everything about it..."

Now It's My Turn

Because of the horrendous experience I had during my son's hospital birth, I was overwhelmed by the fear of repeating that history for the second time, then some 23 years later. As a result I envisioned even worse conditions, and my body responded with obedience to my commands resulting in my blood pressure skyrocketing and our midwife redirecting us from home to the hospital.

After our daughter's birth by caesarean, Peter noted that except for our baby, all the other infants were going without continual skin-to-skin contact during their critical first hours outside the womb. The possible range of side effects for the hospital-born is daunting to consider. Newborns move around for months in the womb. What makes us think they cease being active concurrent to birth? Removing the opportunity for the family to experience the enjoyment of their newborn's antics is uncalled for.

Following Dree's birth, I remained in the hospital for the better part of a week. If you have ever experienced a hospital stay, you understand just how many different nurses I was introduced to. Each one came with the intention of easing my pain with medication. Each one was given the same response, "No thank you! I am breastfeeding!" Believe it or not this did not translate into their language. Some became perplexed, while others grew irate. I felt like the nurses were determined to destroy my newborn child's well-being. And we label this healthcare! Frizzamyer alert!

Finally toward the end of my stay, a nurse came in and sat down to learn why I had been so stubborn. After our encounter she went to her medical database to pull up findings on the safety of the hospital issued drugs. She was convinced that the pain medication all the nurses had been trying so hard to push on me would not harm my child. She told me that I was the only woman on the ward who had refused drugs.

Then when she was unable to substantiate her belief, she began thinking out loud as she compared my baby's response to the others she had tended. She said that the other newborns may have actually been experiencing the same side effects as their mothers with frizzamyers that included irritability and extended crying spells. In our case, many on the nursing staff came into my room just to hold our baby. They all commented on her peaceful disposition. I experienced first hand the importance of my commitment to being a fearless parent in protecting my child's well being no matter who would challenge my authority.

"You can't achieve health through medicine."
Jordan Rubin, N.M.D., Ph.D

The experience of an institutional birth may play a part in the postpartum blues of which many mothers speak. I understand that midwifery and other forms of complimentary healthcare can provide the skills needed to guide couples through the birth process drug free. I see an opportunity for improving the well-being of our institutional births by humanizing healthcare for Mommy, Daddy, and baby.

8

Teach Them to Fail Forward

"I could draw a circle on a piece of paper and Mother made me feel like Van Gogh."
Damon Wayans

Since the time he was two years old, he had been known to fixate on one thing. In fact, when he really got going, he'd rock or even walk back and forth incessantly. He was much more sensitive to sound than any of his peers, to the point that he had to have noises blocked from his hearing. His elementary school teachers were completely frustrated with him. They resorted to calling emergency meetings just to decide what to do with this odd-ball student.

How would you respond to someone like this? What would your attitude be toward this child? Which clinical approach would you choose based on his special needs? And what label would best fit the child just described? If you are thinking "gifted," you are on the right track. The one in question, Jay Greenberg, went on to be a 12-year-old child prodigy studying composition at Julliard.

If Jay were your son and the school insisted that you make immediate changes, where would you have turned for support? How would you have gone about helping him realize his God-given purpose? The attitude we form about a child will greatly influence our interaction with him or her. As a Pre-school and Family Life Coach, I have found it invaluable to learn to recognize the signals a child uses to express his or her need for creative empowerment. In doing so, it is my intent to further a family's goals while leaving their most vulnerable member, the child, completely unharmed.

Another Side of the Elephant

One of my clients told me that she could never be a stay-at-home mom. From the way she described the role, I wouldn't want to be one of those either. Yuck! But what some children need most are much more consistent interactions with family, and one way of ensuring this is to have a primary full-time parent. Having a full time parent will likely involve sacrifice on the whole family's part, but when we as parents can step back and see the big picture—the long term effect of our involvement in our child's life—the rewards of the sacrifice become priceless. Seeing the need for something more in their lives, surprising numbers of families are downsizing their lifestyles in order to restore healthier rituals. Many are being rewarded in "doing" and "having" less and "being" more.

Sometimes, taking a brief sabbatical from the outside world provides us with a unique opportunity for reevaluating our priorities. In today's new global economy, business executives are being forced to do this more and more often. Believe it or not, some owners are now choosing to take time off during the busiest and most stressful times in their industry. By taking such a break and stepping away from what surrounds them each day, they are better equipped to see the big picture, and then choose the best course of action to take in the future.

In the same way, turning off the outside noise enables us to refocus on the business of family. When routine matters have been delegated to those who are well trained and emergency contacts and procedures are in place, taking the time to get out of the fast lane can help us do some much-needed strategizing for our family's success. To this end, I offer coaching retreats so that families can take time away from their routines to construct a working model of what they want their lives to look like, but if something like this is not an appropriate choice for your family at this time, then choose some down time. It is extremely beneficial.

"I know that unremitting attention to business is the price of success, but I don't know what success is."
Charles Dudley Warner (1873)

As a family builder, I thought I should take my advice and re-visit my own priorities. With the pace I maintain, I don't always take time to think about what it is that I do. All I know is that my days fly by. So, I catalogued my activities for a day or two and realized I had left no quality time for my husband! Ugh! After seeing this list, as a couple, we now commit at least 15-minutes of time for each other most days (not including dates and overnight get-a-ways). Do you like how your time is being spent? You might want to consider completing a log yourself. It can help clarify the priorities that you truly want to value the most.

In the Way She Should Go

Did you know that (healthy) four year olds laugh roughly 400 times a day, while adults laugh only 15 to 16 times on average?

What are your top priorities regarding your spouse and children? What do you value most? If you recorded a time log, how accurately did it reflect your answer? Is there any time in there to observe your family dynamic or your children individually? How much time is set aside for your family to interact and bond? Is there time for family dinners, game nights, and other activities? Is there time for each parent to periodically have one-on-one time with each child? I have learned to listen to the spirit of my family's words as much as to the words themselves. As a result we are now enjoying each other's friendship on a fascinating new level.

Just like her brother, our daughter began teaching my husband and me when she was still in utero. When I would put my hand over my belly, she would jump to the opposite side of her play area. But when her Daddy did the same thing, she would become calm and at times fall back asleep. After she was born, Daddy yet had the touch that soothed her. Even as she is now growing, physical touch is still high among her priorities.

Here's what I learned about my daughter during the first few months after her birth:

Love Language Along with physical touch Dree thrived on quality time with me and was attentive to my involvement with her. She studied my movements and mimicked many of my own behaviors. I usually made a smacking sound when I kissed her, and sometimes she did the exact same when she kissed me. When I spoke to her without a smile, she also straightened her facial expression. This was the first love language we shared.

Socially Inclined Dree loved interacting with almost everyone who engaged her and attempted to fight sleep at all costs when others were nearby. Rather than watching the brilliantly colored fish in the aquarium at the library, she watched the people. At only two months, she could move her head to the rhythm as my beautician (whom she adored from the start) sang and danced in front of her. She seemed to thrive by sleeping the most soundly when she knew her mother was near.

Slow to Warm My daughter was a real trouper with the amount of car time she had to endure, but she did not do well without a warning of the events to come. If our trip took longer than was reasonable, she would voice her displeasure unless I comforted her and told here where we were going and what we were going to do. If I moved her in a way that was uncomfortable to her, she would look at me to get a reading on where I was coming from. If she heard an unfamiliar sound, she'd stop whatever she was doing and listen. Once I explained what the sound was, she'd calmly go back to her affairs. While her father was with her nearly 24-hours a day for the first two months of her life, she hesitated to return his affection with endearing coos, even though he had invested large amounts of quality time with her. Except when being calmed, she chose to ease her way into a more intimate relationship with him.

Voracious Learner Within the first 3 hours after her birth, one of our lactation consultants began explaining to me how to breastfeed. We both took note of the baby's posture as she turned her head back and forth between the two of us in the most studious gesture. It was as if she was making sure that she fully understood our plan of action. In this process of experimenting with how to nurse her, I said "big wides" while opening my mouth wide to direct her how to latch on. She immediately mimicked me by opening her mouth the same way in response to my request. This seemed in direct contrast to the words of Friedrich Froebel, the inventor of kindergarten, who said, "Children must master the language of things before they can master the language of words." Hmm! During our daily semi-structured curriculum time, Dree would join in the songs in baby words and even repeat back parts of the song in her own language.

Hyper-Like Mom You may find this hard to believe, but even though we both share this trait, I had to be shown that my daughter was hyper. Sure enough, once this was pointed out to me, I began to notice that my little one was usually only still when she was studying something or when she was sound asleep. This knowledge reminded me of the importance of balancing her character with opposite forms of stimuli. Last night, for example, I massaged her in such a way that my son asked why she was lying there so still. Ah, motherhood at its finest! On the morning we met face to face for the first time, I piled pillows on my lap and held her against my chest. Not yet acclimated to her waterless new surroundings, she attempted her usual uterun acrobatics by seemingly bouncing off those pillows in a vertical leap so high and so fast that it took all I had just to catch her by the legs. To this day the trampoline is by far her favorite pass time. Jumpy! Jumpy!

Variety is Valued I observed that Dree was often least engaged when attending to

> supposedly age-appropriate toys. She much preferred exploring the same things that I was interested in or in finding her own sources of creativity in the grass, trees, herbs, dogs, goats, ducks, music, sports, theater, or as a participant in my business meetings...

These are glimpses of the traits I observed in my daughter early on. I determined to follow her patterns to see how consistent these findings remained as she grew. Now that she is of preschool-age, I have found that for the most part, my initial observations of my child have remained consistent.

After reading this, you are probably thinking to yourself, This gloating mother really stretches things to find the wonder in her child. You are right! My Bible states that we should each approach the kingdom of heaven as a little child (Matthew 18:2-4,OEM), which tells me that there is something extraordinary about these little ones that I would do well not to miss. Knowing that there is greatness inside children flavors how I view every client and most especially my own family. How do you view your children? Your family? How easy or difficult is it for you to get past the mundane, the everyday chores and errands, and see into the heart and soul of your loved ones? It is something for which taking the time, making the time, is one imperative that can enhance your family tapestry overall!

A Miraculous Success Story

I once joined a study group for clinicians and, in most instances, was shunned by them. Their attitude was that my seemingly haphazard methods were somehow inferior to their tried and tested clinical approach. For example, they often sneered at me in treatment team meetings when I would sit on the floor in order to have eye contact with my very young clients—something I do to settle a child's fears of big people and help him or her relax. I have had some lively discourse with clinicians about this adaptation. I've been told it is unprofessional. But I don't know how much more professional I could be when connecting with my precious clients. To whom should I be more responsive than them?

As rookies, many new schoolteachers are given the roughest possible assignments. One county contractor who hired me seemed to subscribe to the same philosophy, as I was fairly new to the more formal field of child behavioral work. After being retained by this childcare provider I found myself inside a system into which most of us would never want to go. Rotating from one residential treatment facility to the next, I was assigned some of the hardest cases to coach.

One residential treatment facility in particular will forever be burned into my memory. From the street, taxpaying constituents would find this building well maintained, but inside it was a whole other world. Walking through the halls for the first time, the place seemed like a prison. The walls were dull and dingy. The children hung around their rooms or cells and stared as I walked by. No one spoke warmly. One of the "inmates" must certainly have had a high profile as her food was put on the floor in the doorway where she ate like an animal. She was barely five years of age. What could she have possibly done to deserve that?

Yet there were some things about this facility that were quite unlike my vision of being incarcerated. In prison, they don't mix the sexes, but here children of all ages and at all levels of dysfunction were co-mingled in these living quarters. And sleeping pills were a standard protocol.

My husband visited a number of Romanian orphanages, and every time he came home he wanted to bring some of the little ones with him. As we swapped stories, I was stunned at the similarities between how our two countries value unwanted children. Romanians apparently still put their children away in honor of their former dictator's regime in which parents were required to fill orphanages rather than care for their children themselves, in order to maintain the work force. Perhaps no one told them that with the dictator long gone, they no longer needed to abandon their children! By contrast, our American society often chooses to send children away voluntarily.

One 14-year old young lady with whom I worked was a system kid for whom frizzamyers abounded. She had been in residential treatment for over a year, had attended a special education classroom, and had received treatment from a psychiatrist, a social worker, a therapist, and others. The facility brought me in on the case because none of these professionals were able to restrain her when she got angry, arrest her provocative behavior, or successfully work with her in any other way for that matter.

When I told the team I was working with I did not want to know the client's case history or diagnosis, I was met with contempt. There seemed to be some kind of code for tattling to which they bound themselves. I explained that I simply preferred not to attach labels to a child whom I had never met. I don't like when it is done to me. In spite of my request not to hear her case history, this particular team just couldn't resist the opportunity to let me know what they thought about this child. They had already labeled her as possibly the most horrific adolescent I would ever encounter. I tried to dismiss every word.

When I finally came face-to-face with this teenager, she was performing a very provocative dance for the young men across the hall from her. Since she was obviously street savvy, I asked her if she was practicing that dance so she could become a prostitute. I knew that this was a risky thing to say, because she had been trained to fight by her father, a professional boxer who had been incarcerated for using his hands as lethal weapons. Most all the adults in her world knew this. So what was I thinking?

When she heard me say this, she moved with deliberation in my direction without a word. Then she stopped and looked deeply into my eyes and, obviously seeing no ill will, suddenly turned and left the room. There were a few more conflicts like this that could have ended with me getting a bloody nose, but this never occurred.

In the short time that we were together, this young girl eventually came to confide in me. She told me that her best memory in life was being in juvenile hall, because it was there that she experienced respect for the first time. Apparently, her teacher admired her interest in learning and took the time to personally guide her studies in mathematics. Would you believe that square roots were her specialty?

It turned out that there was not one thing on record about her character that I found to be true. Professionals had spent a great deal of time analyzing and talking about her, but none had seemingly spent time engaging and listening to her. My coaching gave her the courage she needed to speak up in the treatment team meetings, something she had not previously been willing to do. During one such session, she asked when she might get out, as she hadn't done anything to deserve to be in their system. The authority from the county responded, "I will decide when you get out and if you do! I haven't seen anything in you that lets me know you won't do something wrong on the outside." I cringed at the coldness this authoritarian had toward this precious little girl.

During one of our sessions, this young child went to take a shower and came back much quicker than expected. It turned out that one of the boys had opened the door to her shower and humiliated, she had fled to her room. If you are wondering why she did not see this boy's disrespect to be the result of her own solicitous behavior, consider the analytical stage of a developing adolescent. In a healthy home environment, a teen will test theories about life based on the input they receive from their family. But when a child is denied this vital learning opportunity, it's like being absent from the whole third grade. Whatever stage they miss will remain a mystery to him or her. This need for balance can be restored when the child feels safe enough to begin recouping the loss. Clearly, our client's tax-funded provider was maintaining living conditions that were unsafe to engage beyond basic survival.

When I sat down with the program director to report this sexual abuse, he proceeded to tell me that this was how these kids were and that I'd get used to it after I'd worked in the system long enough. "Haven't you read her file?" he asked. Trying to maintain my composure, I asked him why, since he knew these children's background so well, they had not been separated? He said that I made a good point, but he was not in charge. He told me that he had worked hard to get this position, and wasn't about to do anything to jeopardize it.

In my mind, this caregiver was not just negligent, but was also not providing these children with protection and safety. I found similar abuses occurring in just about every assignment to which this county contractor sent me. I was stunned. After all, wasn't the purpose of placing children in this system to protect them from the atrocities that we determine they should no longer endure in their homes?

> *"We can't solve problems by using the same kind of thinking we used when we created them."*
> Albert Einstein

After climbing the chain of command—all to no avail—I called the regulatory agency in Sacramento and was told even more startling news. The bottom line was that this childcare provider was offering the only game on the block, and without this government contractor, these children would have had no place to go. The system was simply overloaded.

Since I couldn't seem to fit into this child abuse heavy hierarchy, I soon found myself not being assigned any new clients. I was not being fired, only left unassigned to new cases after that. This forced me to ask myself, "Where was my opportunity in all this?" I was face-to-face with one of a child's worst nightmares. I couldn't just hide my head in the sand. This encounter caused my own sense of fearlessness to become much more clearly defined.

Much to her tenacity, my young 14-year old client eventually worked her way right out from under the hold that the county had on her. Through coaching, her attitude became pliable again, and consequently she soon found herself no longer a system kid. Indeed, coaching can be a powerful tool when a person is ready to make the personal investment required. This is even more noteworthy in this case, considering what this beautiful young lady had to overcome.

While this story is probably outside the paradigm of your family experience, it is reflective of what happens to children when we fail to address their frizzamyers—and the balance that can be restored, in even the most extreme cases, when we do.

What value do we assign to our families? What do we find our purpose to be as parents in what was once the wealthiest nation on Earth? We are only as strong as our weakest link.

ADELOGIC Aptitudes

The richest people in the world search out and solve the biggest problems.
Mike Litman

What problem has your child been created to solve? Here is another piece of the puzzle to consider when we evaluate our children's purpose and our own attitudes regarding their learning: There is more than just one kind of **Adelogic Aptitude** in our children. This idea, referred to as "ADELOGIC Sense," takes into account that not all children have the same natural abilities. Some are good with words, while others excel at physical tasks. Some are musical, while others are great with people. Knowing how your child is put together and what his or her strengths are, as well as their weaknesses, and providing them with opportunities for mastery, can give you the confidence to empower your young learner for life.

Various types of Adelogic Aptitudes are given here. This list is still being refined, and you may find that more than one of the characteristics will apply.

Verbal This person is good at describing a concept; may enjoy writing and reading; likes word pictures, puns, rapping, creative phrasing and new words; and enjoys expanding his or her vocabulary.

Exercise: Use tape recordings of his voice, cassettes, and/or CDs of actors describing the material. Join a speech club. This child might just write tomorrow's great American novel!

Visual This individual emphasizes more of what is seen. I even think of those who've experienced the loss of other senses who then develop much sharper visual acuity: like sign language. May use charts and symbols to get a point across, sees things clearly in his or her mind, and can sense what something will look like when completed. A person with this Adelogic Aptitude likes pictures and demonstrations to help understand things.

Exercise: Sketch it. Create a diagram. Envision it. Some home-school parents travel with their children to actually see the places they are studying, providing their learners with embedded recall capability. This child just might turn out to be a renowned architect, cartographer, or city planner!

Physical. This person is a kinesthetic learner, and enjoys the doing, requires a hands-on approach, and is inspired by interacting with the process.

Exercise: Join them in acting out what they've learned. Mime the activity or information. Put it to music. Shadow a professional who engages in a physically active career. Could this child be a future Olympic gymnast, a physical therapist, or even an animal trainer?

Musical This individual remembers commercials, songs, and rhymes, music may well be a focal point for them, normally attuned to timing or rhythm, enjoys and is readily compelled by the flow of things.

Exercise: Share a variety of concerts together: classical, ethnic. Include such performances as Stump, Porgy and Bess, and a host of others. Practice placing your ear on the ground together and you'll soon discover the cadence of life beneath your feet. Find a harpist or even a conductor your child can hang out with for a day. For example, our former piano tuner was reportedly a third generation master of his craft, and if it turned out to be Dree's interest I would seek to expose her to the expertise of just such a craftsman.

Might this child lead a famous rock band, become a classical composer or pianist, win a Tony Award on Broadway, or become a famous mathematician?

Math/Logic This person thinks first with their right brain; arranges things systematically; looks to analyze, and to find the sequence and structure. They may be fascinated with the process of buildings and freeways being constructed along your usual travel route.

Exercise: Fix a favorite recipe using measurements to bring a new concept to life. Build a fort or a tree house together in your yard. Interview a mathematician. Create word problems while planning your garden together, preparing beans for soaking, or grains and spices for grinding... Loosen the rules around how well ordered you like to keep things, and give them a bit more room to experiment with you around the house, also guiding them in the clean up afterwards of course.

Are you raising a child who will find the cure for a dread disease, write the next breakthrough computer program or codes for the CIA?

Introspective A person with this Aptitude thrives having extended time for reflection away from the crowd, evaluates the meaning behind a behavior and may wear you out with the "Why?" of it all, requires time to reflect on new ideas and explore his own reactions to and interpretation of them.

Exercise: Let the classroom extend to the outdoors, the beach, and the mountains. Give them the gift of unhurried time. Ask open ended questions while also allowing time to just be in each others presence. Shut out the rest of the world.

The world is this child's oyster. Everything is interesting, ideas abound. Will this child be an artist, a famous designer, an environmentalist, or a journalist? Whatever he or she does, it will likely come from their innermost soul.

Interpersonal This individual is a negotiator and a peacemaker among men; group dynamics can be a place where this child will find their wings.

Exercise: Attend a workshop, a debate, or another life setting where interpersonal skills are discussed or developed. Engage their input in successfully resolving some of the challenges you face (age appropriately) and also learn from the ones they experience and how they respond.

Are you grooming a budding politician, an attorney, a business magnate, a future Supreme Court Justice, or the president of a college?

Many are the stories I have heard about parents who believed in their children when the professionals were in doubt. Sometimes, it's a different level of giftedness that has the professionals stumped. Sometimes, it's a family dynamic that affects the attitude of caregivers and teachers. But parents who won't give up and who choose to fail forward can find their way through the maze. Their can-do attitude will win out for their child in the end. The same can be true for your little one. Children learn from a variety of experiences, and those who grow through them with the nurturance of their families grow strongest!

"As a child I remember looking under our Christmas tree for my stack of foolscap and a whole box of #2 lead pencils. They were always there, unwrapped.

I got a diary once, but it didn't have enough room to hold all my words, and besides, foolscap was so comfortable.

My uncle was a printer, and I was raised among words. One of my favorite pastimes was to sit on a high stool in his print shop and watch him work. I vividly remember the day I decided to help, so I moved all the type around while he was occupied with a sluggish printing press. When he realized what I had done, he made me sit there through the long night correcting and editing the changes I had made. That night words became a way of life with me, and until I married I helped him edit his assignments."

— Mary Jensen, *Over Salad & Hot Bread*

9

Steer Your Family's Ship into Safe Harbor

Are you a parent who hovers, waiting to solve all the problems you can for your child, particularly disputes between and among your own children?

I cannot count the number of times I've seen a loving parent in the heat of the moment frantically trying to referee a dispute between two opposing sibling. Let's say Kenneth grabs something from his sister, Chelvi, and she screams. While not physically injured, her scream and the pitch she uses are calculated to invoke a fear-based reaction in her parent. The parent then reprimands Kenneth or otherwise reacts.

The result? Kenneth and Chelvi learn that their parent will get involved in solving their discrepancies before they can even consider doing so themselves. If these two were empowered to resolve their own conflicts, the parent may be surprised at how much less dramatic their children's responses might be and how much more enjoyable their family might become. However, in this case, the opportunity for Kenneth and Chelvi to learn how to negotiate a desirable resolution was unintentionally circumvented by Mom or Dad.

There was a time when family doctors made house calls, the premise being that seeing a patient at home provided a glimpse into the living environment that made diagnosing the patient easier and much more accurate. At the start of my coaching practice, I made it a point to provide services in the home environment wherever possible. I found this added tremendous fuel to the effectiveness I had during later phone sessions. So much of the guesswork was eliminated in this way. Even at our best, we miss important family dynamics in a detached clinical setting. By working with families, onsite as a subordinate facilitator, I helped them to effect powerful changes in their lives.

Another Win-Win Scenario

Another example that comes to mind is of a couple of children, who we'll call Tyrell and Michelle, and for whom psychiatry unfortunately played a primary role in their growth and development. On one afternoon, our client's older brother Tyrell arrived home from school with a noticeably disturbed look on his face. Because homework was the first order of business immediately following a full day of public school, the parent directed Tyrell to the study area almost upon entry. Seeing the opportunity to antagonize her brother, Michelle, the younger sibling and our client, took Tyrell's hat and threw it across the room. The young man graciously picked up his hat and sternly called his sister Michelle by her formal name. Not seeing what had occurred, the parent scolded the son for raising his voice.

It was at that point that I gained tremendous respect for Tyrell because he simply responded with compliance. He did not seek to be understood or to share what was obviously bothering him, and neither was he asked. However, Michelle continued finding ways of getting under her brother's skin until he could no longer take it. In response to his frustration with Michelle, rather than going to his parent Tyrell got on his bike to leave the house. At this point, seeing Tyrell about to leave but not understanding why, his parent warned him not to go. Tyrell had reached his limit, so with his best effort at self-restraint, he proceeded to leave without one word of disrespect. His parent, frustrated at having been ignored, grabbed Tyrell by the neck and dragged him over to the phone. The parent called the psychiatrist and said, "Doctor we need to increase the dosage on this child's medication because it is not working!" The physician readily complied. And, having allowed the scenario to play out, this is where I stepped in.

In this instance, the parent was simply overwhelmed and lacked an understanding of Tyrell's motivation. As a coach, I was able to help the parent briefly step outside that stressful situation in order to revisit the long-term outcomes identified earlier. Using "Adelogic Replay" (a technique I developed to review individual scenes in the client's life), the parent was enabled to think about the events that had transpired with greater clarity and without feeling demeaned. Comprehending why Tyrell had acted as he did, the parent realized that the son was behaving with significant restraint. The parent also realized that through facilitative involvement, escalated emotions could be avoided all together. The end result was that the children were allowed by the parent to discover their own voices and were soon well on their way to mastering the art of negotiation and conflict resolution. With fewer fires to put out, this parent was able to begin enjoying not only some much-needed downtime, but also her children.

My Nine Tips for Your Family and Professional Success

It is entirely possible for you as a parent to feel rewarded in your marriage, career, as well as in your child-rearing journey. The following are some tools to help bolster your confidence.

1. **Be an optimist.** Psychiatrist Smiley Blanton states, "I never met a senile person, regardless of age, who did three things: stayed active physically, continued to grow mentally, and developed a genuine interest in other people."
2. **Have a strong team that knows what you don't.** Engage a think tank of carefully chosen people to help you shape your thoughts. This can include family members, your pediatrician, friends, educators. But choose carefully! Take care in shaping your thoughts, because they will also shape you and, by extension, your children!
3. **Have beliefs that are strong enough to commit your life to.** Consider that the same things that work well in your personal life will also work well in your chosen profession.

4. **Remember that when you are challenged, you will automatically revert back to your fundamental beliefs.** Write your eulogy the way you want to be remembered. Then start living every day toward that end result.
5. **Know who you are and the purpose for which you were created.** Ask yourself, Does my life thoroughly fulfill me? Do my family and clients reinforce the value of what I do for them? How excited am I about responding to their honest feedback?
6. **Remember that one of your first priorities as a spouse, parent, or in any other leadership role is to inspire others.** How do those in your care communicate their values to you? How are they asking to be supported? Invest in knowing your team and you will be rewarded with their motivation.
7. **Be an effective communicator.** Hone your observation skills and ask open-ended questions. Be relentless in your preparation and master your subject matter.
8. **Have courage.** Frank A. Dusch states, "You can't stop people from thinking...but you can start them."
9. **Love people.** Wayne Peterson, MBA, states, "A family business that operates on trust, loyalty, and love is the most formidable competitor in the marketplace."

10

Growing A Fear-Free Family

The Family Construct

Parenting is a sacred trust. The majority of us become parents by choice. And once we do, we engage in a whole new level of human experience. What your family dynamic will be is up to you.

What is your ideal picture of family? Does it look like the one you grew up in? If not, how has it been improved upon as you have reconstructed it? How much thought have you given to creating strong family dynamics with positive interaction, great communication, mutual support and respect?

We grow up planning ahead for both ours and our parent's expectations. If we are college bound, we are directed early on in a quest for the grades and activities that will land us on the campus of our choice. And that college is chosen particularly to facilitate getting into the field of our choice. Our lives are strategized and planned so that we can eventually have that four bedroom house with the three car garage. But how much strategizing is done for the family who will inhabit that house? How much thought do we give to just how that family will interact; what its priorities will be; how we can help it be its best?

As parents, we take the lead in making these decisions. Have you developed your family plan—the map that will create a strong family unit with children able to function and cope within the greater society? What are the interactions in your family indicating to you right now?

May I suggest that you sit down and project backwards to before you were parents, to when you were anticipating your first child. When you made that commitment to being parents, what did you want most for your children? Write this down and then assess whether you have or have not reached those goals. Consider whether those goals and ideals are still important to you, and if not, what goals have replaced them.

Parenting is a full-time job. Whatever else you do, whether you are a stay-at-home parent or you engage a different career away from home, you are a parent 24/7, 365 days a year. Do you see yourself as an attuned and responsive role model? Do your priorities reflect this? Most importantly, does your child's behavior affirm this to be true? If your loved ones are clamoring to get to the dinner table to hear about your day and share theirs, if they covet their weekends with you, trust you with their thoughts and feelings, and find security in your interactions with your spouse and with them, your legacy is strong and gaining momentum. Congratulations! It's time to celebrate success and plan for how you'll keep the home fires burning when winter comes. If you are reading this and sensing a need for support in improving your interactions, take heart. You have already taken the first step on your road to success. Here are some additional options for you to consider.

Assess Your Family

- Does your family communicate well and often?
- Do you spend time together both quietly and engaged in mutually enjoyable activities?
- Is there regular, healthy laughter in your home?
- Besides the normal sibling squabbles, do your children enjoy each other?
- Are you approachable?
- Do your children come to you with their concerns and challenges without prompting?
- Do your children observe you and your spouse resolving conflict in healthy ways?
- As your children's parents, do they observe you treating each other with love and respect and making each other a priority?
- Are your children secure in the knowledge that they are also a priority?
- Are your children secure in your love?
- Do your children trust you with their thoughts and feelings?
- Is your home open to your children's friends? And do they see you enjoying yours?
- Are you part of a vibrant community where your values are shared and enhanced?

- Does mutual respect permeate your family life?
- Are your children living up to their social, intellectual, emotional and spiritual potential?
- Are you?
- Do you have a clear handle on your values and have you shared those values with your children?
- Do you teach by example; is your life worth emulating?

If you can honestly say yes to most of the above, you are providing your children with a secure family life. If any of these need work, evaluate where you can make changes so your children and family become a higher priority.

Reminder:
- *The will is most resilient in the face of challenges, and can withstand some of the most crushing assaults.*
- *By contrast, our spirit is as delicate as a rose and can be temporarily crushed if trampled on enough times with the right amount of emotional force.*

A child secure in his parent's love and the strength of his family is a particularly resilient child.

Prioritizing Family

We are a media-driven, technology dependent society. We allow the media to tell us what we should need and want, and technology to provide much of our communication.

More-is-better has become our philosophy, and we are constantly striving to give it to our children: more trips; more gadgets; more things. What they often need is more of us—and our direct interaction with them.

That four-bedroom house with a three-car garage can be a desirable reward. But if scaling down to three bedrooms and two cars means restoring peace in your home, consider it.

As for communication, try a media-free night once a week. Play cards or board games with your kids, read a book together as a family, go for a hike. Do something where you are interacting and communication will follow. Create the opportunities for your family to bond, and make it a regular event that occurs at a consistent time. Your children may object at first, but once they are used to it and can anticipate interaction without pressure, they will relax and really begin to enjoy it.

Shared memories are a huge part of what makes a family close. What are your family's shared memories like? Are there lots of moments of laughter and heartwarming interaction; do you have regular family dinners with great discussions; are you there for the children's sporting events and school programs providing the support they need? Do they know you are vested in their lives, and have you allowed them to be vested in yours?

How do you create your shared memories? They can come from so many things, big and small. Your family doesn't need expensive vacations. Just take them camping—even in the backyard or your living room. Instead of taking the whole family to a movie, have a video and chicken mango salad night together at home. Go to the beach together, create holiday traditions together.

Cook together. Even plant and tend a garden together. Shoot baskets, throw a beach ball around. Think of a new name for your street and solicit the input of others. If the vote is unanimous in some regions, as is the case in ours, the government will actually make it official with a new street sign and soon your mail will come addressed to "Family Place." You'll be teaching your whole community about the power of a few to change the course of history. Splash some paint on an empty wall. Build a fort in your living room. Let your kids choose a family activity. Read together and even write together. There are countless activities you can enjoy that will provide a tapestry of memories that will keep your family close and connected.

> *Why do my parents hate me so much? I get straight A's in college and work to earn my own way, but still they put me down all the time. It hurts so bad! What can I do to earn their respect if not their love?*

A child's self-worth is hugely impacted by their perceptions of their parent's feelings towards them. Our interest in our children's activities, our joy in their accomplishments, our presence when they need us are all ways of showing our children just how important they are to us. Your life may be busy. Your job may be stressful, and combined with all the usual activities of keeping your house running, your family cared for, you may be overwhelmed. But the most precious gift you can give your child is your unhurried time and attention without judging them. Listen to and hear them when they speak—and make time so they can do so. Attend their athletic and school events, and cheer them on. Praise their accomplishments, help them fail forward when they stumble. Laugh with them, sometimes cry with them, and always let them know they are unconditionally loved. Their growth and development are nurtured by the knowledge that you care.

Let your children know they are welcome in your life! And make that welcome unconditional. Children make mistakes; they have foibles; their moods can shift. They need to know that while you welcome them when they are at their best, your arms are open even wider when they need you most. This is no license to abandon discipline. Consistent boundaries lovingly enforced are another way of reassuring our children they are loved.

Take some time to assess your parenting style. Is it an approach to which your child has an enthusiastic response. Were you a child, how would you respond to it?

Socialization is an important part of our lives, and it is an important part of our children's lives. Providing our children with social skills is imperative to their ability to function well in school and in society as a whole. Good manners are the foundation. Have you taught your children to say please and thank you? Are they gracious and considerate? Do they listen without waiting to speak? Are they gracious winners and even more gracious losers? Do they have the ability to share? Do they speak without whining? Do they make eye contact and shake hands when introduced? Are they respectful of the feelings and rights of others? These are just some of the behaviors that will make life easier for them, open more doors of opportunity for them, and help them develop with a strong sense of self worth.

Once again, while we can demand all these behaviors, by setting the example, we truly teach our children both the behaviors and the benefits of them. So ask yourself, "Do I live the example I would like my children to follow?"

How do you handle anger and disappointment? Do you complain and blame others for your misfortunes and failures, or do you own your mistakes? And when you err along the way, do you write it off, or do you apologize? Owning our mistakes and learning from them is so important to emotional and spiritual growth, and setting the example in doing so has a huge impact on our children.

What are your expectations for your children? Are you looking to them for vicarious fulfillment—to accomplish things you wish you had done—or are you celebrating and nurturing their talents, abilities, interests—their unique purpose? Do you talk with your children about their hopes and dreams, inviting them to share them with you? More importantly, can they trust you with them? If, for example, our four-year old tells us he wants to be a forest ranger, a fireman, or drive a big truck, or shares that she wants to be a ballet dancer, a dog walker, or a babysitter, we smile and encourage the fantasy. But if the 16-year-old we think would make a great doctor tells us he or she wants to be a plumber, how do we react? If the child we have provided with golf lessons tells us she really wants to play piano, what do we say? How do we balance guiding our children with allowing them to grow into their own choices?

Our children are a precious gift to us. It is our privilege to nurture them, to love them, and to be loved in return. But they are also individuals whose unique talents, abilities, and needs sometimes try our patience and wear us down.

Optimally, each child would have two parents, one or the other of whom would almost always be available for their care and nurture, balancing out the other's parental extremes. But our world is not an optimal place. Some 50% of marriages end in divorce; many children are now born into single parent families. Blended families abound. In many families, both parents choose to work. But a family is a family, parenthood is parenthood, and once we decide to be parents, it is up to us to be the best parents we can be. We owe that to our children and ourselves.

Every one of us makes mistakes. Our children are wise. They recognize our intentions. They know when they are loved. And they will thrive in all kinds of circumstances if they feel loved, appreciated, supported, and safe. Apologize for your mistakes, but don't dwell on them. As a parent, you are hopefully striving to improve daily. After all, you did buy this book! Just keep failing forward. Give yourself permission to enjoy the journey guilt free!

It is important for families to have support systems. Where extended family once assumed this role, in our mobile society many people live away from the grandparents, aunts, uncles, and others who would otherwise form their village. Thus, parents turn to friends, social groups, educators, doctors, and their churches and synagogues for the practical and emotional support parenting requires. Choose your support systems carefully.

Make sure they share your values, your principles, and that they will honor your parenting style and choices. But accept that no matter how broad your support base, you are the parent and, as such, the ultimate responsibility for your child's welfare rests with you at *www.Fearlessparenting.com.* All card-carrying members who have completed the *Fearless Parenting* series are invited into our online support forum.)

Parents as Guardians and Advocates

As parents, we seek the opinions of others in the raising of our children. We start out by reading books on pregnancy and child care and ask the advice of family and friends. We look to our children's teachers to tell us our children are intelligent, capable, and performing well in school. We ask our pediatricians about their social and physical development and whether it is on target. We are barraged with advice from professionals, and we do well to filter through all of it. In the end, it is our job to use our best judgment and rely on our own instincts in raising our children.

Are you your child's advocate, or do you easily cede your authority to "professionals"? Do you accept a teacher's take on your child's learning abilities, or, having watched your child's development from day one, and after hearing the teacher's input, do you develop your own assessment? When your pediatrician suggests medication for some condition, do you obediently fill and dispense the prescription, or do you ask questions about both its necessity and side effects? Do you look for safe alternatives?

Have you determined that the final decisions regarding your child's well-being, education, social, intellectual, and spiritual direction are yours to nurture? Have you accepted that responsibility?

There is a move these days to begin the formalized educational process earlier and earlier. Many have already bought in, because this is what seemingly unseen forces are demanding. I'm urging you and other fearless parents across the nation to join me in standing up for our children before they belong to the state altogether. In succumbing to this pressure to go beyond our means, and pressuring our children beyond their optimal development, we are losing sight of our real priorities and becoming the cause of some of our children's "frizzamyers."

The pressure is on families to live beyond their means, for our children to achieve more and more, and in our quest to meet these societal standards, we are losing sight of our real priorities and pressuring our children into frizzamyers.

Our children develop at different rates. Some walk earlier, some later. Some talk earlier, some later. Some grow in to social interests earlier than others. While it tends to level out, to expect them to perform within proscribed parameters before they are ready is not only unreasonable, it is potentially damaging. Children know when they are not meeting our expectations, and the frustration concurrent with this leads to frizzamyers. In our fast-paced, immediate gratification society, a child who fails to conform is often labeled. And I am now seeing children of two, three, and four years old labeled with ADD, hyperactivity, oppositional defiance, and a host of other disorders—and our societal response is to then medicate them so they can function within situations for which they are simply notdesigned. Are you proactively seeking to avoid this scenario by allowing your child room to develop at his or her own pace? Are you willing to make the time to help them?

This is not to say we should not challenge our children, and that our expectations for them should not be high. But there is a line between encouraging them to meet their highest potential and pressuring them to fulfill arbitrary expectations. Keep that line clear in your mind, and make sure no one else crosses it where your child is concerned. No one!

Keeping Our Children Safe

As parents, it is our mandate to keep our children safe. On an individual, microcosmic level, this means seeing that they are loved, nurtured, allowed and encouraged to develop to the height of their potential. It means providing them with a home that is a safe haven, a family they can trust with their physical, emotional, intellectual, and spiritual well being.

On a macrocosmic level, it means proactively advocating for both our children and all children; taking an interest in all things that impact our little ones; taking a stand on behalf of not just yours but all children.

Have you taught your child how to deal with strangers without making him or her fearful of everyone? Or is he or she forced to enter the care of one stranger after another as the preschool staff keeps changing? Have you taken the time to know whether child predators reside in your neighborhood, and if they do, who they are? Moreover, do you advocate to protect our children from them?

Do you feed your child a healthful diet, have you introduced him to a variety of nourishing foods, and do you see that he or she gets regular physical activity? Are you advocating to keep soda and candy machines out of your school and physical education in? And if physical education has been cut, as a fearless parent are you requiring that it be brought back?

Have you inspired your child to have a healthy image of themselves, instilling in them strong values by loving them unconditionally and by encouraging them to be the best they can be so that they are better prepared to deflect peer pressure? And are you making sure that your neighborhood and schools are safe havens for them?

Tolerance vs. Actively Engaging the Culture

Children are born with curiosity; none are born bigoted. Children are openly interested and down right curious about others. On the other hand, tolerance has to be learned. Give your children a sense of the world beyond their immediate environment, and they'll quickly understand how interconnected we are on this finite world stage.

Philip M. Harter, MD, asked the question, "If somehow earth's population could have been shrunk into a tiny village with all the human ratios existing in the world still remaining, what would this tiny diverse village have looked like?" Here's an approximation of what his research revealed:

- 30 Christians
- 89 heterosexuals
- 80 in substandard housing
- 50 malnourished
- 1 near death
- 1 pregnant
- 1 college educated
- 70 illiterate
- 1 computer owner
- 6 who possessed 59% of the entire world's wealth, *all* from America.

Bill Gates said, "With great wealth comes great responsibility." Regardless of your family's socio-economic status, just by virtue of living in the United States of America you are among the wealthiest people in the world, and you certainly have tremendous opportunity for even more. So do your children. Teach them about their government, their country, and their contribution to both. Vest them with an appreciation of their heritage in America; and teach them about citizenship. Do it by example. Open the doors and windows of your child's mind to the value of giving out of a thankful heart, while raising them with the strength to hold true to healthy values and principles. There is something powerful about engaging and interacting in dialogue that elevates us all to a higher level of thinking, our children included.

On Parenting...

Parenting is so all encompassing, so challenging in the best possible sense, that no one author could possibly cover all there is to be said about it. The point here is to stimulate your thinking toward more fearless parenting..

Parenting is also a tremendous responsibility that requires an extraordinary time commitment. Parenting can be one of the most fulfilling jobs you will ever have. It vests you with tremendous opportunity for growing and developing alongside your child. As a fearless parent, you can change the world for the better.

I encourage you to embrace your role as the lead contractor on your children's team, and to choose your subs carefully. Engage in multiple interviews with candidates with whom you will contract for your children's well-being—be they doctors, educators, daycare providers, babysitters, or any of a host of others who will impact your children through the years - with even more emphasis on research than you apply when choosing your riskiest investments, your most prized antique collectables, or your next prize winning Arabian or Thoroughbred.

Let your children see your strength and don't be afraid of failure. Show them how skillfully you can fail forward. Be their unfailing advocates. And nourish their spirits with the strength of your love, discipline, respect, and the confidence that no matter how far they reach, they have a strong family to fall back on. In doing so you will not only nurture your children, you will find your voice as well. Do this and I'll meeet you in the winner's circle!

Afterword

"The most fundamental political question is who gets to teach the children?"
— Plato

Many of our preschool children are now being cared for outside the home by professionals we know very little about. Many who end up in preschool are being expelled and consequently labeled and even medicated. And yet the push for mandatory preschool for all remains high.

This book began as a treatise on the topic of preschool for all. However, as I wrote, I realized that so much of what we are as parents is reflected in what compels us to allow others to mandate what we should do with our children. And so this second edition soon broadened considerably in its perspective. However, preschool for all is still on the table, more and more parents are still sending younger and younger children to preschool, and judging by the number of expulsions and drugs prescribed, preschools are still failing to adequately meet the needs of the children they serve. Thus, we still need a dialogue.

The Preschool For All Act, Proposition 82, as it was called, stated that:

> ***Children who were not put in quality preschools fell behind in school and later life.*** But with so few high quality preschools in existence, with the staff turnover in these schools, and with the expulsion rate, how can we truly say that they are effective? Or that they are the only and best way to prepare our children to succeed in school and in life?
>
> ***Preschool is the catalyst for "parent involvement."*** If this is true as Prop 82 stated, why do many parents feel left out of the inner circle? Some express even feeling inferior in schools' authoritarian presence. That was also the tone I detected during the Annual Preschool Director's workshop that I co-chaired for San Diego, and especially during the discussions that I attended that were sponsored by Rob Reiner's group.
>
> ***All California children deserve quality preschool programs taught by well trained teachers using age appropriate curriculum.*** Who decides what is age-appropriate? With preschool-age children developing at such varying rates, how can any one program or curriculum be "age appropriate" for them all? And why are we not considering

> avenues that fall outside of what the state offers such as private programs, family childcare, not to mention the host of other parental choice options including playgroups and all the numerous multigenerational exposures preparing children for life-long learning. Why were all of these developmentally appropriate options excluded?

The fact that the accountability would be based on the "existing preschool system" suggests strongly that the public would have been guaranteed increased incidences of expulsion, and what often follows these expulsions is diagnosing, labeling, and adult medication.

This "one-size fits all" public education model has yet to prove itself successful for every child, especially for those with very special needs. While the Rob Reiner-led push for preschool for all may have been well-intended, it was not well-conceived; it failed to consider the parent as the primary advocate for the child.

Although California voted against this measure by an overwhelming majority, there is another movement afoot. Currently there is a move across California to close all University Child Development departments and fold them into the education department and/or social services. Again, the move would remove the decision-making process from the parents and hand it over to the state. And when this fails, there will be yet another movement designed to wrest control from parents in "the interest of the child."

"You can either try to get inside and have some influence, or you can stay outside and be pure and powerless."
— James Brown

As parents, our mandate is to make responsible, informed decisions on behalf of our children. And we can only do this if we understand all sides of an issue. For example, many parents do not realize that in many communities if a public school team decides that a student is in need of medication to modify behavior, in order to keep that child in school the parent must accede to the medication. Without medication, the child may not attend school, and if the child is not being schooled, the state will take action against the parents. Thus, the parent would seem to have no choice but to medicate the child. Or is there another way? When did we cede this much authority to the state? And how many parents would realize that private school and home schooling may provide viable alternatives?

Parenting is not always convenient. Bucking the system is often even less so. But in the interest of our children, it is incumbent upon us to be aware of what legislation regarding our children is pending, and to make sure that nothing passes that will impinge on our rights as the primary decision-makers for our children. This is what the system is already doing in the absence of our involvement. Whether it is universal preschool or some other seemingly laudable idea, if it in any way weakens our mandate as parents, it is not in the best interest of our children.

"The battle for control and leadership of the world has always been waged most effectively at the idea level."
American Covenant,
Excerpt from John Maxwell's Book,
Thinking for A Change

Institutional education proponents have repeatedly told us about the supposed importance of the "No Child Left Behind" program and "Universal Preschool." But researcher Robert Goodman from the Department of Child and Adolescent Psychiatry at King's College in London told Reuters that regardless of when children start school, the youngest in the class always struggle more than the rest. Apparently, Goodman was finding a noticeable increase in mental illness as a result. It turns out that starting formal education later might be the wisest investment after all. For the state of the children, it seems that the handwriting is on the wall.

What the Pilot State Is Saying

In an exclusive interview that I conducted with the Georgia family childcare community, I tried to get a sense of just how our providers down South were viewing the "Preschool For All" (Pre-K) movement, now that it is in place there. These were a few of their thoughts:

> "Many of you know my position on this topic. It's been a very sore one for me! Parents need options for where they feel is the best placement

for their child. Is a large group of 20 right for every child? What about the brain research that shows that children learn best with small groups of emotionally involved adults?"

"I have to disagree with this on some points, having four of my own children go through the Georgia lottery… frankly, being in a very small home… with infants/toddlers is a bit stifling to their social growth."

"Gee! Are you saying FCC [Family Child Care] providers should just roll over and allow the thinking that FCC is not of quality and that centers are better? I'm thrilled for your children that are doing so well and went through pre-K… On the other hand, FCC also produces very good students. It does take planning and structure. Most of my children stay with me thru their pr-K years and they also excel…"

"We [at FCC] go to events… such as puppet shows and book times at the library… as well as taking ballet and soccer and religious classes… taking turns being line leader, speaking… helping set the table and cleaning up… waiting in line at the bathroom and washing hands… using both gross and fine motor skills…."

"My child is in Pre-K… this year. We put her there for the socialization part of it. I personally feel like it has slowed down her learning though…."

"As many of you know, all of my clients are teachers, most in elementary schools… I am

> fortunate in that they see the downsides to the Pre-K program...."
>
> "At one time, it was discussed about adding qualified family child care homes to the mix but as you know it did not become a reality...."

Regardless of which side of the fence they found themselves on, these folks had strong opinions. How sad that for most Georgia families, the choice appeared to have been removed from them.

The one-size fits all public education model has not proven successful for every child, especially for those with very special needs. So shouldn't we be putting our tax dollars where they would be of the most use?

What Our Lead Spokesperson Had to Say

Serving on our local family childcare board for a short time, I learned how frightened most of these providers really were about the future of the early childhood industry. It turned out that many were running from the field or bowing to the strong arm tactics of the new union, because they did not see any way of keeping their home-based ventures alive. And this is despite the fact that they represented the largest small business sector in the county!

In 2003, I attended a presentation on Preschool for All for Head Start employees. During the presentation, legitimate concerns were raised by the staff about programs that would not meet Department of Education standards. Betty Bassoff, Ph.D., and lead spokesperson for Rob Reiner's movement at the local level, responded to their corporate misgivings this way: "As these things go, Preschool for All will eventually become compulsory, and programs not meeting standards (family childcare, private preschools, faith-based programs) will be left behind." In Universal Preschool Programs: A Review of the Literature, she further states:

"Opposition is predictably from the conservative right element in communities, focusing on questionable benefits to middle class children (no research supporting) new public funding commitments, expanding bureaucratization of public education at earlier and earlier ages, undermining of the maternal-child relationship, suspect outside influences, fear for mandatory enrollment."

"The uncreative mind can spot wrong answers,
But it takes a creative mind to spot wrong questions."
— Antony Jay, Excerpt from John Maxwell's Book,
Thinking For A Change

I first became interested in school outcome statistics after attending an end of the year school board meeting for our area. One of our charter schools was designed specifically to support home school families, and their achievements were included in the board's agenda. Mind you, students who were primarily taught by their credential-free parents represented less than one percent of those being educated but as I observed events unfold that evening, they scarfed up more than three quarters of the awards in both math and science as compared to those educated in neighboring institutional settings. Regardless of your choice of instruction, let me challenge you to stand tall as you involve yourself in your children's development, and in exercising your right to choose.

Parental investment has consistently been our children's strongest predictor of success. Not surprisingly, the importance of our influence at home cannot be overstated. Take just this one chart for example. Most of us do not have teaching credentials, which makes these school readiness findings quite remarkable, especially for minorities:

Statistical Outcomes	**Home School**	**Public School**
Avg. Reading Score - White	87 Percentile	61 Percentile
Avg. Reading Score - Minority	87 Percentile	49 Percentile
Avg. Mathematics Score - White	82 Percentile	60 Percentile
Avg. Mathematics Score - Minority	77 Percentile	50 Percentile

Source: Center for Education Reform

The New York Times slandered charter schools for being ineffective despite a whole host of data to the contrary. Conversely, in December 2004, a Harvard University study found that charter school students were more likely to be proficient in reading and math than students in neighboring conventional schools. The greatest achievement gains were seen among African American, Hispanic, or low-income students.

"The great masses of the people...will more easily fall victims to a big lie than to a small one.
— Adolf Hitler, *Mein Kampf* (1924), 1.10

As parents, we must remind ourselves that the government is meant to work for us. We pay the salaries of government employees. We hire and fire our elected officials with our votes. And we influence them with letters, phone calls, and petitions. As with all other aspects of our children's lives, it is imperative that we remain vigilant about the educational process. That we volunteer in their schools, mentor a struggling student, stay active in our communities, keep aware of proposed changes in the educational system, raise our voices when those changes might negatively impact our children, and financially support those who truly advocate for our families. It is our right and our responsibility to join forces in walking our children right out the front door of schools and other systems that undermine our parental right to choose. And it is our imperative in this critical hour in U.S. history that we begin to do so..

"A good civilization spreads over us freely like a tree varying and yielding because it is alive.
A bad civilization stands up and sticks out above us like an umbrella—artificial, mathematical in shape, not merely universal, but uniform."
— G.K. Chesterton,
"Cheese" Alarms and Discussion (1910)

Postscript

At the very core of my unique approach lies a fundamental interest in restoring peace to the otherwise wounded human spirit, especially the spirits of children. Many techniques do embrace cognitive, social, and even emotional constructs. Each certainly adds value. We are fast advancing our understanding of our own function. Yet none of these channels explain the power of the human spirit to overcome unimaginable hardships including abuse and neglect, life threatening dis-ease, war, famine, hopelessness, depression, torture, and so many other vicissitudes of life.

We rightly recognize leaders in the sciences, literature, humanities, politics, entertainment, sports and other disciplines for their noteworthy accomplishments. Common courtesy dictates that we do so. Thus, I feel compelled out of common courtesy, if nothing else, to recognize the Source of the successful track record being ascribed to my life's work. While I can claim my education as a contributor, no university text author can have the method attributed to their efforts. No past or present theorist, nor any of the current protocols being used on children with behavioral issues can be assigned its just reward. Instead, it is my irrevocable privilege to acknowledge the One who is repeatedly setting the captives free. I get chills considering that Yeshuah the Messiah (Jesus Christ) would entrust such miraculously transforming, child-tested trade secrets to me, yet as you have witnessed within these pages He has done exactly that! And I am truly honored.

I am most grateful to you for your purchase of this book, and I pray that what you have found within its pages inspires you as a parent and that your family continues to benefit from your having read it. Now flip back to the Adelogic Action Plan at the beginning of the book and take the first steps in creating the family you've dreamed of. You're just that powerful!

Recommended Reading

Trillion Dollar Moms, by Maria T. Bailey and Bonnie W. Ulman

Over Salad and Hot Bread, by Mary Jenson

Spirit Warrior, by Peter Zindler. A Christian science-fiction adventure of a boy in outer space. Awarded the Reader's Choice Award.

Seeds of Greatness Planted in the Heartland, by Peter Zindler. A compelling discourse to challenge you to higher heights in your faith.

The Coaching Revolution, by David Logan, Ph.D., & John King

Grace Based Parenting, by Dr. Tim Kimmel. Dr. Kimmel is author of *Raising Kids Who Turn Out Right: Set Your Family Free*

What Babies Say Before They Can Talk, By Paul C. Holinger, M.D., M.P.H. The nine signals infants use to express their feelings.

GLOSSARY

Cesarean By shortening and altering, surgical operation through the walls of the abdomen and uterus for the purpose of delivering a baby.

Clinical Applying objective or standardized methods to the description, evaluation, or modification of human behavior. Based on or involving medical treatment, practice, observation, or diagnosis

Cognitive Based on or capable of being reduced to empirical factual knowledge.

Complementary Health Care A therapy or system of non-medical modalities aimed at maintaining optimum health

Health Care Nurturing an optimum state of wellbeing.

Concrete Operations Piaget's theory that children aged 7 to 11 years are capable of understanding the world in terms of reason rather than in terms of naïve perception.

Cops and Crops A computerized video game curriculum chosen by public school administrators, which can promote criminal and/or otherwise defiant behavior in students

Depakote Used in the treatment of mania, associated with bipolar disorder.

Disease Lack of ease, an impairment of the normal state of the living animal or plant body or of any of its components that interrupts or modifies the performance of the vital functions.

Emergent Curriculum A learning opportunity that is developed out of a circumstance and/or based on the interest of the student.

Enuresis Urination on one's self

Frederick Froebel German educator who founded the kindergarten system.

Frizzamyer An appropriate need signaling child behavior. An unusual way in which a person expresses the existence of an unmet need.

Health The state of being sound in body or mind, flourishing condition, wellbeing, vitality.

Homeopathy A system of medical practice that treats a disease by the administration of minute doses of a remedy that would in healthy persons produce symptoms of the disease treated.

Kinsey, Alfred Zoologist and child pedophile from Indiana University who is regarded by many as the foremost pioneer in the quantitative study of human sexuality. Also author of *Sexuality in the Human Male*, in which he boasts heinous accounts of sexually torturing infants and children with full funding from many prominent American institutions, including the Rockefeller Foundation. (For info visit: http://www.drjudithreisman.com.)

Lactation Consultant	One skilled in instructing a mother in how to nurse her infant.
Life Coach	Professional coach who provides ongoing partnership to help clients produce fulfilling results in their personal and professional lives and to improve performance and enhance the quality of their lives. A life coach is trained to listen, observe, and customize their approach to individual client needs, seeks to elicit solutions and strategies from the client, believes the client to be naturally creative and resourceful, and provides support to enhance the skills, resources, and creativity that the client already has.
Love Languages	Dr. Gary Chapman's five ways of expressing devotion and commitment that can be learned or changed to touch hearts. These include (1) words of affirmation, (2) receiving gifts, (3) spending quality time, (4) performing acts of service, and (5) physical touch.
Manipulative	Of, relating to, or performed by manipulation—treating or operating with the hands or by mechanical means especially in a skillful manner
Mayo Clinic	A world-renowned medical practice operated by the Mayo Foundation, a non-profit organization based in Rochester, Minnesota.
Meltdown	The process or course of melting something (now associated with a noticeably altered or diminished emotional state).
OEM	Original equipment manufacturer.
Osteopathic Pediatrician	Licensed physician having a degree in osteopathic medicine. This can be a family physician or a specialist who utilizes the scientific method to diagnose and treat patients, offers a balanced system of health care to cure as well as prevent disease, emphasizes caring for the whole person, and can provide an added dimension to their patient's healthcare through osteopathic manipulative treatment (OMT).
Pavlovian Model	Russian physicist who observed conditioned salivary responses in dogs and imposed his theory on humans.
Pharmacy	Drug, medicine, poison, or magic potion used to practice divination or magic. The art, practice, or profession of preparing, preserving, compounding, and dispensing medical drugs.
Piaget	Swiss psychologist remembered for his studies of cognitive development in children.
Post-partum blues	Range of often confusing emotions that can be felt by a parent following the addition of a new baby to the family.

Pre-operational Piaget's theory that children from 2 to 7 years tend to literally believe what they see.

Prozac Any of a group of drugs that inhibit the inactivation of serotonin by blocking its absorption in the central nervous system. Often used as antidepressants.

Seroquel™ One of the atypical anti-psychotics. Seroquel™ is the trade name for quetiapine. Quetiapine has FDA and international approvals for the treatment of schizophrenia and acute mania in bipolar disorder. It is used "off-label" to treat other disorders such as post-traumatic stress disorder, obsessive-compulsive disorder, and as a sedative for those with sleep disorders.

Slow to Warm Character trait in which the person engages with others cautiously.

Spirit An animating or vital principle held to give life to physical organisms. a person's non-physical being, composed of their character and emotions. Life-giving element of a natural body.

System Kid A child who is a ward of the courts or a resident of the government-sponsored system of care.

Treatment Team Group usually comprised largely of medical professionals who consult with clinical methods in treating needs that are often emotional and/or spiritual in nature.

Titration A process of making mixtures of decreasing amounts of one substance, usually in solution with unvarying amounts of another until a mixture which contains the smallest amount of the substance still produces the desired effect.

Very Special Need Yearning inherent in human nature, characterized by the need for improving one's circumstance.

Vioxx A drug that was being used for pain relief and was being studied for its ability to prevent cancer and to block the growth of new blood vessels to solid tumors. It belongs to the family of non-steroidal anti-inflammatory drugs.

Will To be inclined to do something, choose, or consent. Used to express determination.

FEARLESS PARENTING

Raising Your Child
with
Confidence and Purpose

Read other reviews.

Tell us what you think.

Purchase the
Fearless Parenting Audio Series

Sign up for Club Fearless—The Blog

visit:

www.FearlessParenting.com